MURDEROUS

The MAGIC of MATHS

Kjartan Poskitt

SCHOLASTIC

www.murderousmaths.co.uk

Scholastic Children's Books,
Euston House, 24 Eversholt Street,
London NW1 1DB, UK

A division of Scholastic Ltd
London ~ New York ~ Toronto ~ Sydney ~ Auckland
Mexico City ~ New Delhi ~ Hong Kong

Published by Scholastic Ltd, 2014

ISBN 978 1407 14720 8

Printed and bound by CPI Group (UK) Ltd, Croydon, CR0 4YY

2 4 6 8 10 9 7 5 3 1

CONTENTS

KJARTAN POSKITT's first jobs included playing pianos very loudly, presenting children's tv, inventing puzzles and writing pantomimes. Maths was his best subject at school, because it was the only one that didn't need good spelling and handwriting. As well as 30 maths books, he has written books about space, magic, codes and pants, and he also writes the Agatha Parrot and Borgon the Axeboy books. His favourite number is 12,988,816 because that's how many ways you can put 32 dominoes on a chessboard (although he didn't count them himself). If he wasn't an author he would like to have been a sound effects man. He has two old pinball tables, seven guitars and lots of dangerous old music synthesisers and he plays all of them… badly!

THE MIDNIGHT CLOCK

Look over your shoulder.
  Is there anybody watching?
No? Good.

How would you like to be a mind reader? Or tell people's fortunes? Or play games that you can't lose? This book is going to show you how to do a whole range of tricks to amaze and fool people, bul right now we'll start with a nice little trick just for YOU.

This is Thag our Murderous Mathematician and he has a magic clock.

It always takes you to midnight!

You'll see that the odd numbers are all in squares, and they are in the right place. The even numbers are in circles, but some of them have been moved round! Here's how the magic works.

Pick any number. Move round the clock that number of places. Whatever number you finish on, you move that number of places.

It doesn't matter what number you start on, you'll always end up at midnight!

(If you start on an even number, you'll land on midnight straight away, then when you move 12 places you come back to midnight!)

You can draw this clock out and decorate it to make a big spooky version! Remember — it's just like drawing a normal clock, except you swap the 2 and 10, and you swap the 4 and the 8. It would make a great decoration for Halloween ... *wooo!*

Now you've seen a little trick, let's get you started properly...

What will you need for this book?

The best thing about maths tricks is that you don't need a lot of expensive stuff. The main things you need are:

- Pencil and paper
- Calculator
- A pack of playing cards*
- Scissors
- Some coins
- An elephant. (A fully grown giant African elephant is best but an Indian elephant works just as well.)

---

* Some tricks need you to use a NINE PACK. All you do to make one of these is take an ace,2,3,4,5,6,7,8 and 9 from the pack. The ace counts as 1.

So, go and get the pencil and paper and cards and scissors and coins and an elephant out of a cupboard, and we're all set to go! The only other thing you'll need are some friends. In this book we're going to use Daz and Nancy, but you can use anybody you like.

How hard are the tricks?

Some tricks are easy, but some of the maths in the cleverer tricks gets a bit murderous. Here's a useful guide.

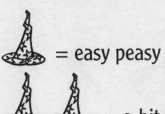 = easy peasy

= a bit tougher

= murderous – but worth it!

Of course you can always start on the easy tricks and then if you like them, you can get going on the hard ones.

For some of the tricks you need to cut shapes out of paper. You can find printable sheets as well as some extra ideas and explanations at:

www.murderousmaths.co.uk/magic

BEAT THE CALCULATOR

Calculator tricks are brilliant because nearly everybody has got one. Some people just have normal calculators, but you also find calculators on computers, phones, rulers, pencil cases ... gosh, soon we'll have calculators on socks and cornflakes. So go and find one and let's do some magic!

The Calculator Test

The first thing you need to do with any calculator is test it. All you do is put in 12345679 (you have to miss the 8 out). Then you push ×9 = and you'll immediately know if your calculator is a good ONE. (You'll see why ONE is in big letters when you try it.)

Just for fun, instead of putting in ×9 you can use any number in the nine times table, such as ×27 or ×63.

How to make a calculator friendly

Push these buttons:

2×2×2×2 = ×3×3×3×3 = -2-3-2 = ×2×3÷100 ÷100 =

Turn the calculator upside down and look at the answer!

The 7, 11, 13 trick!

Pass a friend a calculator – we'll use Daz – and ask him to put in any THREE digit number he likes, and then show you what it is. Then, as fast as he can, he has to push:

×7×11×13 =

You will have already written the answer down before he's finished!

All you do is write Daz's number down twice. So if Daz puts in 571, the answer will be 571571. Test it out yourself if you don't believe it!

The reason this works is that $7 \times 11 \times 13 = 1,001$. When you multiply any three digit number by 1,001, you just get the same number twice. Neat, isn't it?

If you like this trick, here are a few more. Try them yourself on a calculator and see what they do!

Put in a TWO digit number then push:

$\times 3 \times 7 \times 13 \times 37 =$

Put in a single digit then push:

$\times 3 \times 37 =$

Put in a single digit then push:

$\times 3 \times 7 \times 11 \times 13 \times 37 =$

The Missing Digit

Ask Daz to push any four digits he likes on the calculator except 0, then push ×9 =

He should have a five digit answer (unless he pushed 1111, but if he did then he's lazy so give him a PROD and tell him to try harder.)

Daz reads the first four of the digits of the answer. You can tell him the last digit!

The Secret: If you multiply any number by 9, then the digits in the answer will always add up to a number in the nine times table. If you try 2759×9 you get 24831, and then you'll find 2+4+8+3+1 = 18, and of course 18 is in the nine times table.

If Daz had said 7, 8, 4, 2 you would just add them up. 7+8+4+2 = 21. The next number up in the nine times table is 27, so what do you need to add on? It's 6 … and that would be the missing digit!

The Magic 37

Choose any number from 1–9, and push that button three times, then push the DIVIDE button.

In your head, add up the digits you can see on the screen. Put the answer in.

Push =

It doesn't matter what number you pick to start with, the answer will be 37!

The Two Twos Trick

For this trick you'll need your NINE PACK (see page 8) as well as a calculator. You'll also need two more "twos" from the rest of your pack of cards.

Before you start, lie the two twos face down on the table. Tell Daz he's going to do a mystery sum, and these cards have the answer!

Shuffle the nine pack, then ask Daz to pick three of the cards. He has to use the numbers on them to make six different two-digit numbers.

Write them out in a column and add them up with the calculator.

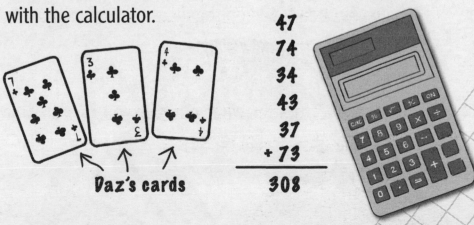

```
  47
  74
  34
  43
  37
+ 73
─────
 308
```

Daz's cards

Now add up the three numbers on the cards, then divide the answer into the other answer.

$$7+3+4 = 14$$

$$308÷14 = 22$$

Turn over the face-down cards to show Daz the two twos!

The Calendar Race

Get a calendar that shows a whole month at once.

Draw a rectangle around any block of TWENTY numbers.

				1	2	3
4	5	6	7	8	9	10
11	12	13	14	15	16	17
18	19	20	21	22	23	24
25	26	27	28	29	30	31

Give a friend a calculator (we'll use Nancy) and see how fast she can add all twenty numbers up...

...but you know the answer straightaway!

The Secret: All you do is add the smallest number to the biggest number then multiply by 10. Here you get 4+29 = 33, then 33×10 = 330. This will work with any block of 20 numbers on any month!

Now that we've done a few little calculator tricks, it's time for a BIG one...

The Amazing Big Prediction

This trick seems absolutely impossible but all you need are a few *nine bonds*. They're simple. You start with any digit, and write down what you need to add to make 9. So if you start with 2, its nine bond is 7 because 2+7 = 9. You can try it with a long number and write the nine bonds underneath like this:

85023
14976

The sneaky bit is that when you add these two long numbers you get 99999, and that's the secret bit of maths that makes this trick work!

Practise your nine bonds until you can do them really quickly, then it's time to open the theatre, get the audience in and click on the lights for SHOWTIME!

Get Daz up onto the stage. He'll probably need his calculator, but all you need is a big pen and paper plus your elephant and some glittery trousers. (Actually you don't need the trousers, but it's nice if you can make the effort.)

Start off drawing a grid with five lines of five squares, then an extra line with six squares.

Ask Daz to write any five different digits he likes across the third line. If he writes 42157, it would look like this:

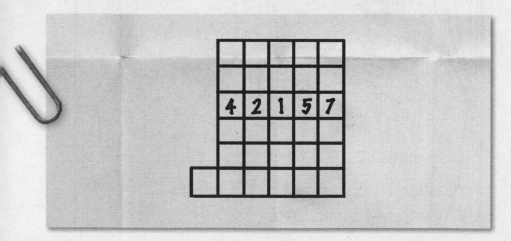

At this point you write a secret prediction on a piece of paper. Fold it up, then put it on the floor and let the elephant stand on it, so that everybody knows you can't cheat. Remind everybody that so far Daz has only filled in one line of the grid!

Now ask Daz to fill in the top two lines with all the digits from 0–9. He can put them in any order he wants.

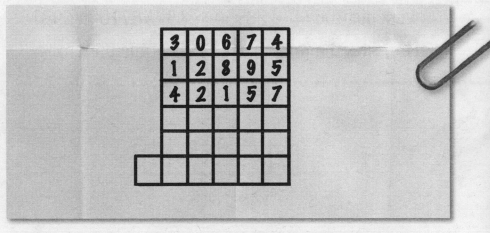

Tell everybody that you're going to fill in the next two lines with all the digits 0–9.

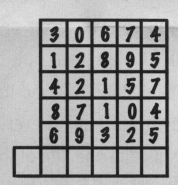

Next you ask Daz to add up the five big numbers! He might need his calculator because he has to work out 30674+12895+42157+87104+69325. He writes the total in the boxes at the bottom.

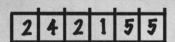

You then ask the elephant to open up your prediction and show everybody...

Then you do a big bow while everybody cheers and screams and goes crazy. Wahey!

How to do it...

There are two parts to this trick. The first part is when you write down the prediction. At that point Daz had only written down 42157. Whatever number you see there, all you do is put an extra 2 on the front and subtract 2 from the end.

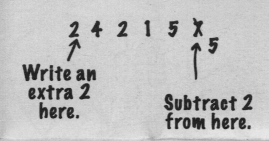

2 4 2 1 5 X

Write an extra 2 here.

Subtract 2 from here.

5

The second part is when you fill in your numbers 0–9. Look at the top and bottom lines of the grid, then look at the second and fourth lines. It's just those nine bonds you've been practising. If you do them quickly enough then nobody will realize you're doing some sneaky sums. After that, the maths does the magic for you!

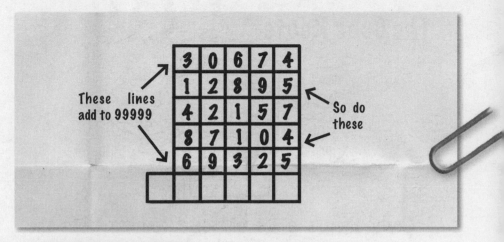

These lines add to 99999

So do these

How does it work?

After Daz has written down his number, all that happens is that two lots of 99999 get added to it. The number 99999 is the same as 100000 − 1, so if we just added 99999 to Daz's number, we'd just need to put a 1 on the front and subtract 1 from the end! But this trick adds on *two* lots of 999999, so that's the same as putting 2 on the front and subtracting 2 from the end.

Tah-dah!

The Cube Rooter

Gosh, there's a lot of noise coming from the basement of the Murderous Maths building. That's where our utterly nutty Pure Mathematicians do their experiments. Maybe they've invented a two-cornered triangle? Or have they found a box full of spare decimal points? Perhaps they've calculated a number that smells of chocolate? Let's have a look...

ANSWER TO PAGE 207
When you start, the cards are in order going clockwise round the edge. The only way to get the joker in the middle is if you put the cards in order going ANTI-clockwise round the edge. Challenge a friend to try it!

28

Aha! They've been practising the cube root trick. It's exactly the sort of thing that utterly nutty people love.

A cube number is what you get when you multiply the same number by itself three times. So 6×6×6 = 216. You can say 216 is the *cube* of 6. You can also say it the other way round: 6 is the *cube root* of 216. And if you don't want to write out 6×6×6, you can just write 6^3. The little ^{3} means you write out the 6 three times and multiply them together.

For this trick, somebody picks any two digit number and works out the cube on a calculator. If they picked 51, they would put 51×51×51 = and the answer would be 132651. They then tell you the answer, and you can tell them what number they started with!

To do it you need to know the cubes of the numbers 0–9.

Number	Sum	Cube
0^3	0×0×0	0
1^3	1×1×1	1
2^3	2×2×2	8
3^3	3×3×3	27

4^3	$4 \times 4 \times 4$	64
5^3	$5 \times 5 \times 5$	125
6^3	$6 \times 6 \times 6$	216
7^3	$7 \times 7 \times 7$	343
8^3	$8 \times 8 \times 8$	512
9^3	$9 \times 9 \times 9$	729

There are two little jobs to do, so let's ask the Pure Mathematicians to give us a nice cube number to play with.

We need to separate off the last three digits so we get 19 and 683. The 19 will tell us the first digit of the answer, the 683 will tell us the second digit!

First we get 19 and compare it with the cube numbers on our table. It comes in between 8 and 27. We pick the *smaller* one of these numbers which is 8, and that is the cube of 2. This tells us that the first digit of our answer is 2.

Next we get 683. We only need to look at the last digit, which is 3. Now look at the cubes table. Which cube ends in 3? It's 343, and that is the cube of 7.

There's the answer – the cube root of 19683 = 27.

Try another!

How about 314432?

Easy. We split it into 314 and 432. To get the first digit we see 314 comes in between 216 and 343, and the smaller number is 216, which is the cube of 6. For the second digit we see that 432 ends with a 2, and the cube of 8 ends in a 2, so that's the second digit. The answer is 68!

Like we said, you have to be utterly nutty to love this trick, but some people ARE utterly nutty. In fact, for our Pure Mathematicians, life is just one big party.

The Poisoned Chocolate Bar!

Two people are sharing a bar of chocolate marked into squares. They can both see that one square is poisoned! They take turns to break off a strip of chocolate and eat it. The strip can be wide or narrow, but it has to be broken all the way along any one of the lines. The idea is to force the other person to eat the last poisoned square!

Here's what happens…

So how can you be sure that the other person eats the last square?

This is a nice game to play with a friend such as Daz. You don't need to use real chocolate and poison, you can just use a rectangular piece of paper. Get a pencil and a ruler and divide it up into as many squares as you like. 7×8 is a good number. Ask Daz to mark one of the squares as poisoned.

You then take turns to "break off" strips of chocolate by folding the paper along the lines and then cutting along the folds.

There are two ways to help you win this game.

1 Put the poison in the middle! When it's your turn, see if you can fold the paper in such a way that the poison is exactly in the middle. If you can do that, then whatever Daz does next turn, you can put the poison back in the middle again.

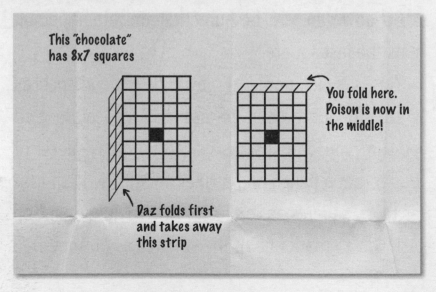

This "chocolate" has 8x7 squares

Daz folds first and takes away this strip

You fold here. Poison is now in the middle!

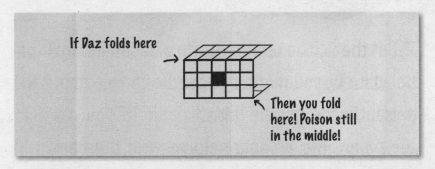

If Daz folds here →

↖ Then you fold here! Poison still in the middle!

You'll see here that when Daz took two lines off the top, you just took two lines off the bottom. The poison went back in the middle and there was NOTHING Daz could do about it. If you keep putting the poison in the middle, the game will probably end with you passing Daz three little squares like this:

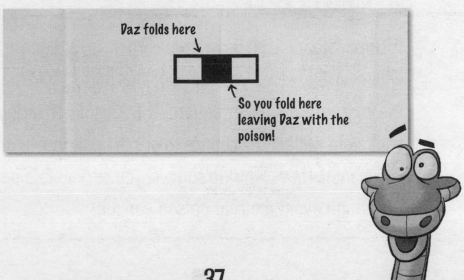

Daz folds here ↓

↑ So you fold here leaving Daz with the poison!

2 Put the poison on the corner of a square. If Daz is being lucky, you might not get the chance to put the poison in the middle. Don't panic! If you can fold the paper into a square shape with the poison in the corner, you will still win!

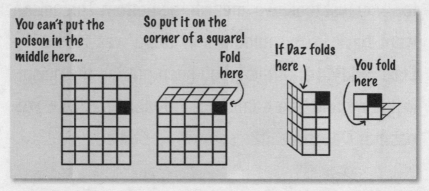

You can't put the poison in the middle here...

So put it on the corner of a square! Fold here

If Daz folds here

You fold here

Once the poison is in the corner of a square, whatever Daz does you can put the poison back in the corner of a smaller square. If Daz is VERY lucky, you might not get the chance to put the poison where you want it. That's why we suggest you stick to folding paper and avoid the real poison version!

THINK OF A NUMBER

There are lots of different *Think of a Number* tricks. We'll start with a couple of easy ones, and then see if you want to try something a bit more murderous!

The Magic 3

This is a good time to use your elephant. Paint a big number "3" on it then make it lie down behind the sofa and call Nancy in.

Shhh!

Hi! What did you want?

Ask Nancy to try this: think of a number. (The trick works with any number, but it's easier if the number is less than 10.)

Add 2
Multiply by 5
Add 3
Multiply by 2
Add 4
Divide by 10
Take away the number you first thought of.
What's your answer?

Now tell your elephant to come out from behind the sofa

I don't believe it my answer IS three!

Incidentally, if your elephant is busy, you can always just tell Nancy her answer is 3 after she's done the sums.

The Hidden Dice

Pass Nancy one or two dice. She throws them but doesn't let you see how they landed! (If you haven't got any dice, Nancy can just think of a number between 1 and 12.)

This is what she has to do:

Add 1 to the score on the dice.
Times by 2
Take away 3
Times by 5
Tell you the answer.

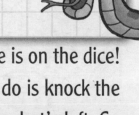

Now you can tell Nancy what score is on the dice! Suppose Nancy says "35". All you do is knock the 5 off the end, and then add one to what's left. So for 35 you knock off the 5, and then add 3+1 to give the answer 4. Try it yourself and see!

Think of TWO numbers!

You can use this trick to dazzle people with numbers. That's why Pongo McWhiffy is using it to find out more about the terribly lovely Veronica Gumfloss.

This is what Pongo asks Veronica to do…

Put in 13
Multiply by her weight in kilograms
Subtract 13
Multiply by 7
Subtract 10
Add her age
Multiply by 11

Take away her weight
Take away her age
Add 101
Tell him the answer.

How did Pongo work out Veronica's details from the number 54160? All Pongo had to do was knock the zero off the end. (That gave him 5416)

For her age, he added one to the last two digits (16+1 = 17)

For her weight he added one to the front digits (54+1 = 55)

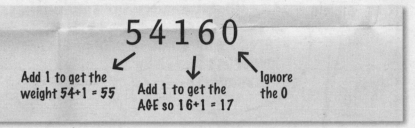

You can try this trick on anybody, or you can even test it on yourself! You can choose any two numbers. It could be the day and month of your birthday, or how many socks and shoes you have, or even how many pounds and pennies you have.

Hunt The Alien Picnic!

We now have a very special *Think of a Number* trick to show you, but it relies on some unwilling volunteers. Aha! Here they come now. It's the Evil Gollarks from the Planet Zog.

Perfect! We'll let them go, then we can hunt them down with a bit of maths magic! While they're setting off, you have to think of a number between 1 and 9.

Ha ha! That's what THEY think. Now get a pencil and paper and do this:

Add 20 to your number
Multiply your answer by 2
Add 119
Multiply by 5

The answer should have three digits. CROSS OUT the middle digit to leave a two digit number.

Turn to that page in the book!

MAGIC SQUARES

If you go into Thag's spell room, look on the wall next to his Midnight Clock. You'll see this nice little magic square.

If you add up any straight line of three numbers going across, down or diagonally, you always get 15. There are eight ways to do this!

Thag can change it so that it adds to any number in the 3 times table. Watch this.

All he's done is taken 1 away from every number, and this time it adds up to 12. The square could even make numbers lower than 12, but Thag would have to put in some minus signs, so we won't bother him with that.

We'll just ask him to change his magic square once more…

What do you think the lines on this square add up to?

It's easy to work out. Just look at the number in the middle and multiply by 3!

The Big Magic Square

Thag has got an even bigger magic square carved out on his floor.

17	24	1	8	15
23	5	7	14	16
4	6	13	20	22
10	12	19	21	3
11	18	25	2	9

This one adds up to 65 along all the straight lines! You can also add the four corners and the 13 in the middle to get 65.

There's a really neat way of drawing this square out. You start with an empty grid, and put 1 in the middle square at the top. You then work diagonally upwards, filling in the numbers 2, 3, 4, 5 and so on. If you go off the top, you come on at the bottom, and if you go off the side you come on the other side. Here's how it starts:

		1		
	5			
4	6			
				3
			2	

Once you get to 5, you can't go any further because the 1 is in the way, so you put the 6 under the 5 and continue. Keep going and you'll finally fill in all 25 numbers!

You can make magic squares of any size you like but right now we're going to see the mad one that Thag keeps locked away in his basement!

The DEMON Square!

This magic square might not be the biggest, but it's the best!

15	4	5	10
6	9	16	3
12	7	2	13
1	14	11	8

It has all the numbers from 1–16 and it starts off being nice and sensible. If you look along any straight line, the numbers add to 34. There are four lines going across, four lines going down and two diagonals. That makes ten ways so far, but now it's all going to go MAD.

You'll find that the four corners add to 34, and so do the four in the middle. If you split the whole square up into four small squares, the numbers in each one add to 34 … in fact this magic square works in TWENTY FOUR different ways!

Are you ready for this?

Here they all are then…

Here's the good bit. You can make your own demon square add up to almost any number you like! You just have to change the numbers 13, 14, 15 and 16 in the shaded squares.

15	4	5	10
6	9	16	3
12	7	2	13
1	14	11	8

The numbers 1-12 never have to change!

At the moment the demon square works for the number 34. Suppose you want it to work for the number 41? 41 is 7 bigger then 34, so all you do is add 7 to the four shaded numbers. This is what you get:

22	4	5	10
6	9	23	3
12	7	2	20
1	21	11	8

You'll find that the demon square now makes 41 in twenty four ways!

This makes for a really impressive trick. All you have to do is remember where the numbers go in

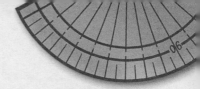

the first demon square. Ask somebody for a number. Suppose they say 23? That's 11 less than 34, so you just take 11 away from the shaded numbers. (Your demon square might end up having a few numbers the same but that doesn't matter.) If they say 49, that's 15 more then 34, so you add 15 to the shaded numbers.

But are 24 ways of making your demon number enough? No of course not!

If you want an extra four ways, then draw a big letter H on your grid and make the arms stick out!

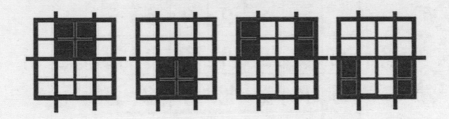

The Magic Calendar

It isn't just Thag who has magic squares in his house. You might have some magic squares hanging up in your kitchen!

All you need is a calendar which has a whole month of dates showing on one page. You can use it to make a completely different sort of magic square, so get Daz in and give him a pencil. He is about to be AMAZED.

Ask Daz to draw a square box around any NINE numbers.

		1	2	3	4	5
6	7	8	9	10	11	12
13	14	15	16	17	18	19
20	21	22	23	24	25	26
27	28	29	30	31		

You now write a prediction on a piece of paper, and tell Daz to put it in his pocket.

Daz then has to draw a ring round any number in the box, then cross out the other numbers in the same row and same column. If he chose 11, it would look like this:

		1	2	3	4	5
6	7	8	9	10	11	12
13	14	15	16	17	18	19
20	21	22	23	24	25	26
27	28	29	30	31		

There are four numbers left, so he puts a ring round one of them (16) and crosses out the numbers in the same row and column.

This just leaves one number (3), so he puts a ring round that one too.

59

		1	2	3	4	5
6	7	8	9	10	11	12
13	14	15	16	17	18	19
20	21	22	23	24	25	26
27	28	29	30	31		

Ask Daz to add the three numbers with rings round them. (3+11+16 = 30)

And now … ask him to take the piece of paper out his pocket and see what you wrote!

Pick Daz off the floor because he will have fainted in amazement.

So how did you know?

All you need to do is look at the middle number in the square and multiply it by three. (In this case 10×3 = 30)

The best thing is that this will work with ANY month, and it doesn't matter where Daz draws the square as long as it goes round nine numbers.

If you're feeling clever, you can do the bigger version. Get Daz to draw a square round any 16 numbers, then you write your prediction. Daz puts rings round numbers, and crosses out the rows and columns as before. Here's how it might look when he's finished:

				1	2	3
4	5	6	7	8	9	10
11	12	13	14	15	16	17
18	19	20	21	22	23	24
25	26	27	28	29	30	31

Ask Daz to add the four numbers with rings round them. Here he'll get 5+14+22+27 = 68 ... which is exactly what you wrote on the paper!

How did you know?

You add up the numbers in the four corners. Or if you prefer it, just add up the biggest number and the smallest number then multiply the answer by 2. You'll get the same result!

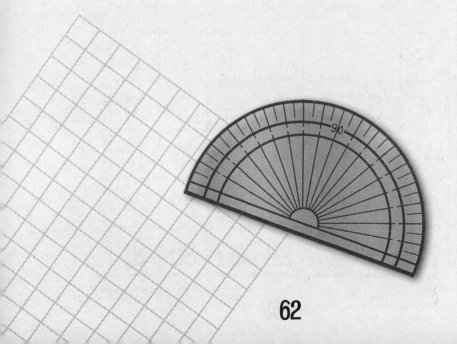

CARD TRICKS

For these tricks you'll need a pack of playing cards. A full pack has 52 cards, and these are divided into four suits called spades, hearts, diamonds and clubs.

The Line Up

You show Nancy that you have 6 cards. They are ace, 2, 3, 4, 5, 6 but they're all mixed up.

You can put them in order without looking, just by counting!

Hold the cards face down in your hand.

Say "one" then turn the top card over and put it face up on the table. It's the ace!

Count "one, two" and as you do so, put the top card to the bottom of the pile, then turn the second card over and put it face up on the table. It's the two!

Count "one, two, three" and put the top card to the bottom, then the second card to the bottom then turn over the third. It's the three!

In the same way count up to four to get the four, then to five to get the five, and finally your last card will be the six!

For this trick to work you need to start with the cards in the special order. Ace, 4, 2, 5, 6, 3. (Look at the picture to check!)

You can even do this trick with TEN cards. The order you need to start the cards is ace, 8, 2, 9, 7, 3, 10, 5, 6, 4.

The Scrambled Cards

Here's a simple little trick to practise. You need an ace, 2, 3, 4, 5, 6. When you've got this to work, you'll be able to do something really strange!

Tips:
• When you deal the cards, you must put one card on each pile in turn, starting with pile A.
• When you stack the piles, always do it in order with pile A at the bottom.

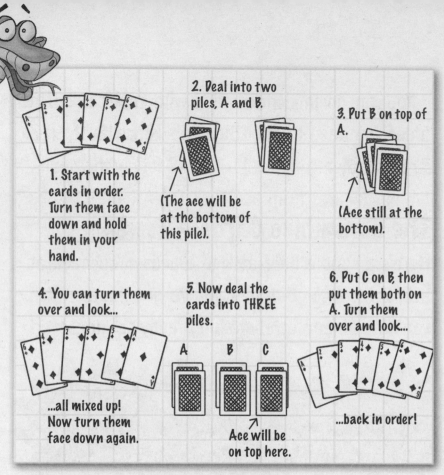

2. Deal into two piles, A and B.

3. Put B on top of A.

1. Start with the cards in order. Turn them face down and hold them in your hand.

(The ace will be at the bottom of this pile).

(Ace still at the bottom).

4. You can turn them over and look...

5. Now deal the cards into THREE piles.

6. Put C on B, then put them both on A. Turn them over and look...

...all mixed up! Now turn them face down again.

A   B   C

Ace will be on top here.

...back in order!

So why do the cards mix up and then go back in order? It's because we had six cards, and dealt them into two piles, then three piles. 2×3 = 6. If you like you could deal them into three piles first, and then two. It would still work.

You can do this trick with any number of cards that divides. Try it with 15 cards! Start with ten red cards in order from ace to 10, and follow them with five black cards from ace to 5. Deal them into five piles, stack them together then turn them round and see them all mixed up. Then turn them back and deal them into three piles. Stack them together, turn them round and they will be back in order! That's because $5 \times 3 = 15$.

Now you're ready to do a really impressive trick!

Get an ace, 2, 3, 4, 5, 6, 7, 8, 9, 10, jack and a queen and put them in order.

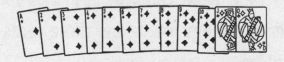

Put them face down and deal them into three little piles of four cards each. Stack up the piles. If you turn them over and look at them they should be in this order with the ace on the top and the queen on the bottom.

(If you don't want to deal the three piles, you can just put the cards in this order to start with.)

You also need three extra cards from the pack, a 2, 4, and a 6.

Now go and find Nancy and give her the three extra cards.

Show her the twelve cards are all in the wrong order.

Ask her to put any one of her three cards face up on the table.

Suppose Nancy puts down the SIX, deal the cards into six piles and then stack them up.

Ask Nancy put down another card. If it's the TWO, deal the cards into two piles and stack them up.

Ask Nancy to put down the last card, so if it's the FOUR, deal four piles and stack them up.

Turn the cards over and show Nancy.

They will all be in the right order!

It doesn't matter what order Nancy plays her three cards, this will always work!

Why? Because $3 \times 4 = 12$ and also $2 \times 6 = 12$. This trick scrambles and unscrambles the cards twice!

The Five Card Trick

If you've got an old pack of cards with a few missing, this trick is perfect. You're going to make some special cards with numbers on both sides. Here's what you need:

Five RED cards: Ace, 2, 3, 4, 5

Five BLACK cards: 6, 7, 8, 9, 10.

Some glue.

Glue the red cards back to back with the black cards like this:

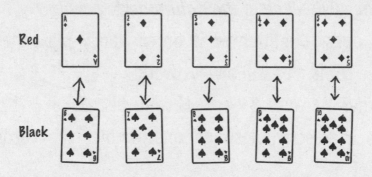

If you don't have any old playing cards, you can always use five blank bits of card and write the red numbers on one side and the black numbers on the other.

When you've made your cards, pass them to Daz. You can then turn round or wear a blindfold, or if you like you can stand behind your elephant so you can't see anything.

Ask Daz to mix up the cards then throw them in the air. When they land on the floor, ask him how many BLACK numbers he can see. You can tell him what all five cards add up to without looking!

You can ask Daz to flip one or more cards over, and then tell you how many black cards there are. You'll be able to tell him the new total!

Even though it will fool Daz, it's a very easy trick.

Suppose Daz says there are NO black cards. The five red cards add up to 15. (Ace counts as 1.) If he says there is ONE black card, it doesn't matter which card it is, the number on the back is 5 more, so the total will be 15+5 = 20. The other totals are easy to remember if you know the five times table:

Number of black cards	0	1	2	3	4	5
Total of all cards	15	20	25	30	35	40

The Late King

The Queen of Hearts is lying face up on the table. You have seven cards in your hand face down. You explain that the Queen is waiting for the King of Hearts, but he is always the last to turn up!

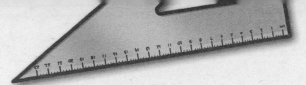

1 Ask Nancy to choose any number between one and six. Let's assume Nancy says FOUR.

2 Take one card at a time from the top of the pack and put it at the bottom keeping it face down. Count as you do so: one-two-three ... but when you get to the FOURTH card, turn it face up. It won't be the King of Hearts, so put it at the bottom, still face up.

3 Repeat step **2** five more times, counting up to four each time, until there is only one face down card left in the little pack you are holding.

4 Spread the cards out on the table. Turn over the last face-down card. It's the King of Hearts!

The Secret: Start with the King of Hearts at the bottom of your seven cards, and the trick works itself. It doesn't matter what number Nancy picks between 1–6, all the other cards will turn over before the 7th and last card!

This nice little trick works with any prime number[*] of cards, so you could try it with eleven cards if you like, and Nancy can pick any number from 1–10.

Whatever number you pick he's ALWAYS last!

The Four Aces

For our last card trick we'll ride on down to the Last Chance Saloon where Riverboat Lil and her 52 little helpers are working their magic on Brett Shuffler.

---

* Prime numbers are numbers that you can't make by multiplying two smaller numbers together.

Lil puts the ACE to the side of the table then puts the rest of the cards back on the old pile and starts again.

Lil's Secret:

Before you start, you have to secretly set up the deck of cards. The pack should all be face down. The top nine cards can be anything, after that you put in the four aces, and then the rest of the cards go underneath. You then play the trick exactly as Lil did with Brett, and it should work itself.

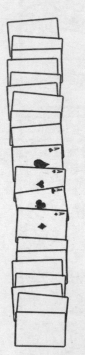

If you want to practise, put the four aces in facing upwards. When you're counting the cards out, you'll be able to check where they are and make sure you're doing it right.

How Does It Work?

Imagine these are your cards.

Pick a number between 11 and 19 and count down from the top. Then add the digits and count back up (starting with the card you finished on). You will end up on the ace of spades!

Now pretend the ace of spades has gone and repeat the trick, picking a different number and missing out the ace of spades when you're counting. You'll end up on the ace of hearts!

Keep going and you'll end up on the other two aces.

Where's the Joker?

You need all the aces, 2s, 3s, 4s, 5s, 6s, and 7s from a pack of cards, plus one joker. (If you don't have a joker you can use a jack or queen or king.) Count the cards and check you've got 29 in total.

Hold the joker and let Nancy shuffle the other 28 cards. Nancy then passes the pack to you face down, and you put the joker face down on top. Take off a small pile of cards and put them on the table.

Take off a small* pile with JOKER on the top ↘

(*The secret is to take SIX cards!)

Pass the rest of the pack to Nancy. She can split it into five or six piles any way she likes and set them out on the table.

You then tell Nancy to "bury" the joker. She picks up her piles in any order and puts them on top of the joker pile. You're going to find the joker using some number magic!

Pick up the pack and turn the cards over one by one dealing them onto a face-up pile. As you do so, ask Nancy to count down "Five, four, three, two, one…"

If you happen to turn over a card with the same number as Nancy just said, then leave it face up on the top of the pile. You then start a new pile counting down from "five" again.

If you count all the way down to one and there hasn't been a matching number, then put one more card face down on the pile to cover it up. (So the pile will end up with six cards.) Start a new pile counting down from five again. Keep going until you have got four piles.

If you're very unlucky then all four piles will have got a face down card on top. You need to start the dealing again, but hold on to the cards still in your hand! Turn all the cards in the four piles face down, shuffle them together and put them back on top of the cards you are still holding. Deal out the four piles again.

If you can see one or more numbers on top of the piles, add them up.

Count off cards one by one from the rest of the pile you are holding. When you get to the number you worked out, turn the card over. It's the joker!

$$2 + 1 + 5 = 8$$

← Cards left in hand.
Joker will be 8th card down!

The Secret. This trick almost works itself. The only clever thing you have to do is at the start of the trick. When you take off the small pile of cards, secretly count them. Make sure the pile has SIX cards with the joker face down on top. It doesn't matter how Nancy splits up the rest of the pack and piles it up, so long as the joker ends up being the 6th card from the bottom, the trick will work!

The Seven Cards of Devious Trickery

The richest man who ever lived was the Great Rhun of Jephatti, and here is just one of the many tales told of his fabulous wealth.

The Great Rhun invited the Prince of Gullabal to a feast of fifty courses, and then he suggested that they played a game at which the prince could not lose.

The prince had to put 100 gold coins on the table. The Rhun had seven cards. The backs of the cards were all gold, but on the other side, four of the cards were black and three were red. When the game started, all the cards were mixed up then laid out on the table with the gold side upwards.

"You will bet half your money, then turn over any card," said the Rhun. "If it is a black card, I will give you 50 gold coins. But if the card is red, you will lose 50 coins."

But even though there were four winning black cards and only three losing red cards, the prince did not trust the Great Rhun. Therefore the Rhun made the game even more tempting.

"Do not fear losing," he said. "For we shall play seven times and each card will be turned once. Each time you bet half your money. You will be sure to win four times, and yet lose only three!"

At last the prince agreed to play and sure enough, he won four times and only lost three times.

BUT … at the end of the game the prince was left with 63 gold coins, and the Great Rhun was 37 coins richer!

How could the Rhun get richer by losing?
The key to this trick are the two rules:
1 All seven cards must be played.
2 The prince bets half his money every time.

The best way to see what happens is to play this game yourself. Get four black cards and three red cards, put them face down and mix them up. Get a pencil and paper to keep your score and write 100 at the top.

Here's what might happen.

You bet half of 100 which is 50. Turn a card.
BLACK! You win 50 so your score is 100+50 = 150.

You bet half of 150 which is 75. Turn a card.
RED! You lose 75, so your score is 150-75 =75.
(Notice that you've won one time, and lost one time, but already you are down to 75. It would be the same if you'd lost first and then won.)

You bet half of 75 which is 37·5, but we'll round it to 38 to make the sums easier. Turn a card.
BLACK! You win 38 so your score is 75+38 = 113.
Keep going until you've played all seven cards.

It doesn't matter what order you play the cards in, you will always end up with a score of about 63. If you happen to have a friend with 100 gold coins, play this game and you'll win around 37 coins every time!

THE CLEVEREST TRICK
IN THIS BOOK

We're going to start by practising a classic old card trick, and then we're going to do something really unbelievable!

The Classic 21 Card Trick

You need 21 cards from a normal pack. Let Daz choose one without you seeing, then put it back. He can then shuffle the cards.

Hold the cards face down, then turn them face up one by one and deal them into three piles, putting one card on each pile in turn.

Hold cards FACE down

Turn cards over one by one and deal into three piles

Daz has to watch without saying anything, but then after you've finished, ask Daz which pile his card was in.

Stack the three piles on top of each other, but make sure the pile with Daz's card goes in the middle!

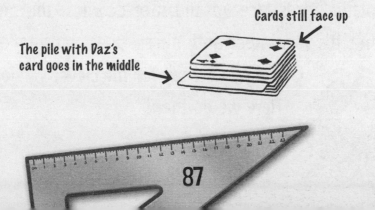

Cards still face up

The pile with Daz's card goes in the middle →

It doesn't matter which way round you put the other two piles. Pick up the stack of cards and turn them all face down. Repeat the process of dealing the cards into three piles, then stacking the piles up two more times. Each time make sure the pile with Daz's card goes in the middle. Always remember to turn the cards face down when you pick the stack up, then turn them face up one by one as you deal them.

After you've stacked the piles up for the third time, pick up the stack and turn it face down. Deal off the top ten cards, then turn over the 11th card. It will be the one Daz chose!

Practise this trick a few times, making sure you've got the cards face up and face down at the right time. It's very important!

OK, are you ready for the clever version? Here we go then!

The 27 Card Trick

This time you start with 27 cards. Daz chooses a card, which he keeps secret, and he also chooses a number from 1–27, which he tells you at the start of the trick. You're going to deal the cards into three piles three times, but then you're going to count through the pack to Daz's number, and that's where his card will appear ... even though you have no idea what his card is!

This trick is truly awesome, and well worth a bit of practise.

You deal out the 27 cards in exactly the same way as the classic 21 card trick. The clever bit is working out how to stack the three piles up. As soon as Daz tells you his number you have to do a few quick sums!

Subtract 1
Divide by 3. Remember the remainder!
Divide the answer by 3. Remember the remainder!
What's left?

Suppose Daz says 16, this is how the sums work out:

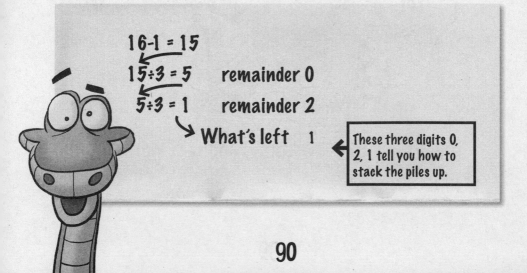

16-1 = 15
15÷3 = 5   remainder 0
5÷3 = 1   remainder 2
        What's left   1

These three digits 0, 2, 1 tell you how to stack the piles up.

You'll end up remembering three digits, in this case it's 0, 2, 1.

These digits tell you where you should put Daz's pile in the stack.

0 = BOTTOM
1 = MIDDLE
2 = TOP

The first digit was 0, so that means after the first deal you stack up the cards with Daz's pile at the *bottom*.

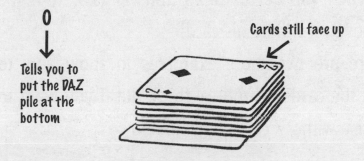

0
↓
Tells you to put the DAZ pile at the bottom

Cards still face up

Pick the stack up, turn them face down and deal them out into three piles again. Daz tells you which pile his card was in.

The next digit you remembered was 2, which tells you to put Daz's pile on the *top* of the stack.

Once again, pick the stack up and turn it face down. Deal out three piles and ask Daz which pile his card was in. The last digit was 1 which tells you to put Daz's pile in the *middle* of the stack.

Finally, pick the stack up and turn the cards face down. Deal them off one at a time counting as you go. When you get to Daz's number (16) turn the card over. It will be his card!

Here are two more examples to show how to stack the cards up. You try these out if you want to practise with 27 cards by yourself.

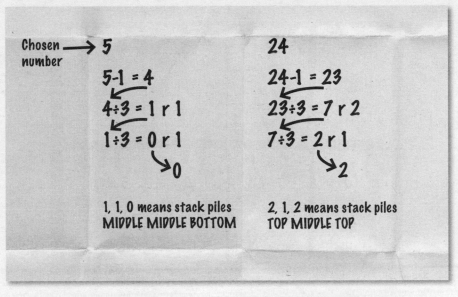

Chosen number → 5

$5-1 = 4$

$4÷3 = 1 \text{ r } 1$

$1÷3 = 0 \text{ r } 1$

↘ 0

1, 1, 0 means stack piles
MIDDLE MIDDLE BOTTOM

24

$24-1 = 23$

$23÷3 = 7 \text{ r } 2$

$7÷3 = 2 \text{ r } 1$

↘ 2

2, 1, 2 means stack piles
TOP MIDDLE TOP

Good luck with this one. It's tricky, but it's worth it

All in Order!

You need eight small pieces of card or paper numbered 1–8. If you've got a pack of old playing cards with some missing, you can use eight of them!

Each card needs to have three holes in the top, so if you've got a hole punch that's perfect! Most of the cards need the holes turning into slots like this:

If you haven't got a hole punch, you can cut three slots into *every* card, then put a bit of tape or a sticker along the top to turn some of the the slots into holes where needed.

Now you shuffle the cards up, then hold them with their backs to you. All the holes and slots should be at the top. Get a thin stick or a nail and do this:

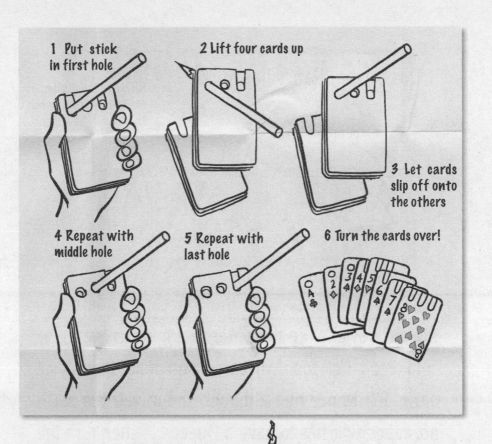

1 Put stick in first hole

2 Lift four cards up

3 Let cards slip off onto the others

4 Repeat with middle hole

5 Repeat with last hole

6 Turn the cards over!

Kings and Queens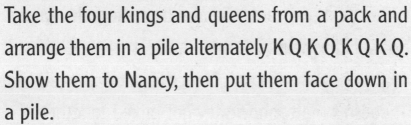

Take the four kings and queens from a pack and arrange them in a pile alternately K Q K Q K Q K Q. Show them to Nancy, then put them face down in a pile.

This is what Nancy has to do:

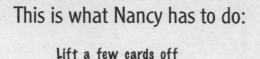

Lift a few cards off
and put them down

Push the two piles of
cards together to mix
them up

(Don't let Nancy slide the top card underneath the pack or change the order in any other way!)

Take off the top two cards and hold them face down. Tell Nancy that although she mixed the cards up, every King has to have a Queen ... then turn the two cards over to show there IS a King and Queen!

The next two cards will also be a King and Queen, so will the next pair and the last pair! It doesn't matter how many cards Nancy lifted off the pile and it doesn't matter how they got mixed together!

You can do a big version of this trick with the whole pack. Sort the cards so they go red-black-red-black all the way through, then split them into two piles and either push or riffle shuffle them together. Every pair of cards starting from the will be one red and one black!

The Predictor Cards

This trick needs the special set of four cards shown on page 98. You can copy the page from the book onto a clean piece of paper then cut the shapes out.

Three of the shapes are squares, but you have to cut the grey areas out too. The fourth MASTER card is twice as wide. You cut it out in one piece and then fold it backwards down the middle and glue it. You should end up with a square card with numbers on both sides.

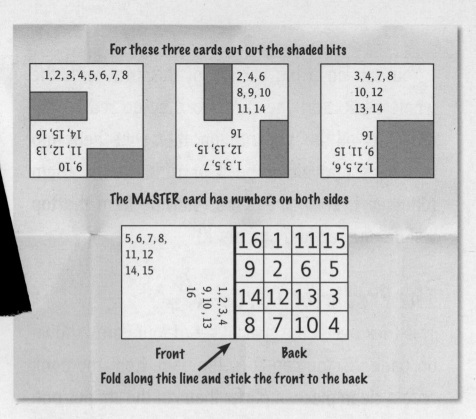

For these three cards cut out the shaded bits

1, 2, 3, 4, 5, 6, 7, 8

9, 10
11, 12, 13
14, 15, 16

2, 4, 6
8, 9, 10
11, 14

1, 3, 5, 7
12, 13, 15,
16

3, 4, 7, 8
10, 12
13, 14

1, 2, 5, 6,
9, 11, 15
16

The MASTER card has numbers on both sides

5, 6, 7, 8, 11, 12 14, 15	1, 2, 3, 4 9, 10, 13 16	16	1	11	15
		9	2	6	5
		14	12	13	3
		8	7	10	4

Front   Back

Fold along this line and stick the front to the back

The Trick

Ask Nancy to choose a number between 1–16. Lay the cards out with the master card front side up.

Nancy has to turn the cards round so that her number is the right way up on the top. Suppose she chooses the number 3, the cards will look like this:

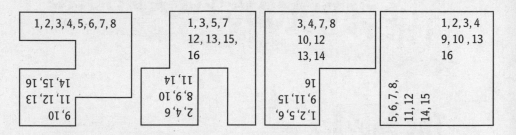

1, 2, 3, 4, 5, 6, 7, 8

14, 15, 16
11, 12, 13
9, 10

1, 3, 5, 7
12, 13, 15,
16

11, 14
8, 9, 10
2, 4, 6

3, 4, 7, 8
10, 12
13, 14

16
9, 11, 15
1, 2, 5, 6,

1, 2, 3, 4
9, 10 , 13
16

5, 6, 7, 8,
11, 12
14, 15

Now you stack the cards up with the MASTER card on top!

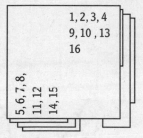

1, 2, 3, 4
9, 10 , 13
16

5, 6, 7, 8,
11, 12
14, 15

Oh boy, are you ready for this? Now turn the pile of cards over and you can see Nancy's number through the hole at the back!

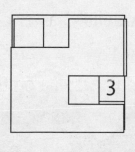

3

THE FABULOUS FLEXAGONS

The Babyflex

Here's a little square thing with four 1s on it. On the back there are four 2s.

FRONT

BACK

Now watch carefully!

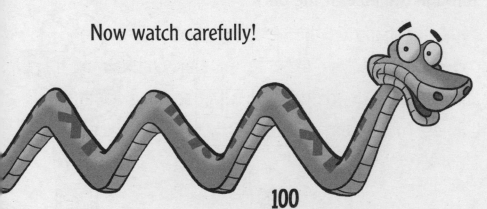

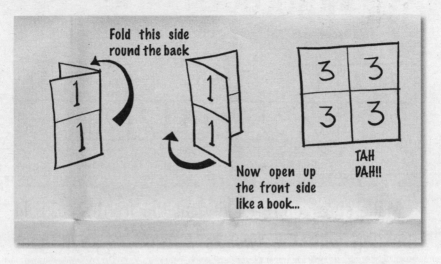

Fold this side round the back

Now open up the front side like a book...

TAH DAH!!

Four 3s have appeared! There are no little secret doors or flaps involved, it's just a simple piece of paper with a complicated name. It's a *tri-tetra-flexagon*.

How to make it:

Copy the shape on the next page onto a piece of paper, cut it out, then draw the numbers on the front and the back. (If you've got a bit of squared paper, it'll help you get the lines in exactly the right place.)

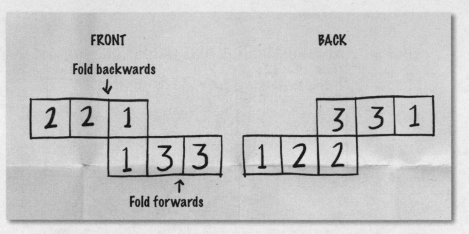

Make sure you're looking at the front side. Fold the flap with the two 2s *backwards* so it goes underneath the 1. Fold the 3 forwards so it lies face to face on top of the other 3.

You should end up with all four 1's on the front. Stick a bit of tape across the two 1's on the right hand side:

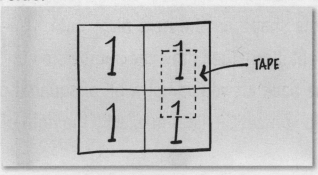

That's it! Now just fold it and unfold like we did on page 101 to make the four 3s appear.

The good thing is that you don't have to draw numbers on your little flexagon. Pongo McWhiffy made a lovely one for Veronica Gumfloss with flowers on the outside then a surprise picture inside.

When you've got the little flexagon to work, have a go at making our awesome Flexamonster!

The Flexamonster

You show Nancy a flexagon with a picture of an evil alien on it.

Then you flip the flexagon around a couple of times and pass it over. See if Nancy can find the alien again. It's really hard unless she knows the secret!

This trick uses a *HEXA-tetra-flexagon!*

At first it looks the same as the little Babyflex we just made, but instead of three faces, this one has six. (A face is what we call a flat side.) When you start flipping it you can find four of the faces quite easily, but there are two more *secret* faces!

Start with a square piece of paper (or thin card). Use a ruler and pencil to divide it into sixteen small squares. You can do this by folding the paper carefully then drawing lines along the folds.

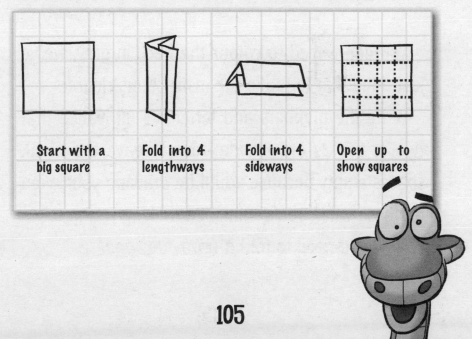

Start with a
big square

Fold into 4
lengthways

Fold into 4
sideways

Open up to
show squares

Cut out the four middle squares and leave a cut in the side to make this shape.

You don't need to colour the back in grey, we've just done that to make the instructions clearer.

Write the numbers and letter 'x's in. Notice that two of the 2s are upside down! Leave the blank spaces empty because you'll be drawing your alien on these when you've finished making it.

Now you need to fold it up.

Start by looking at the BACK of the paper.

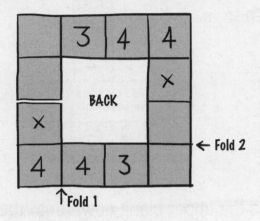

1 Fold the 4 in the bottom corner over onto the 4 next to it.

2 In the other bottom corner, fold the upper blank square down onto the lower blank square. That will bring the whole top bit down.

Turn the whole thing over and you should end up with this:

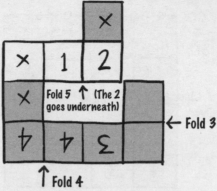

3 Fold the upper blank down onto the lower blank.

4 Fold the right hand 4 over onto the 4 in the corner.

5 Fold the 2 at the top *backwards* so it tucks round underneath the 1.

How are you doing?

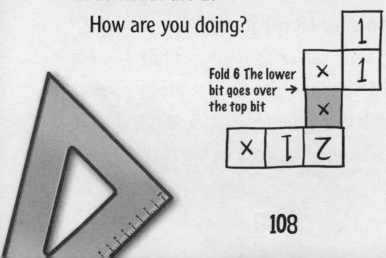

6 Fold the bottom half up across the middle so that the lower x goes onto the upper x.

You're nearly there!

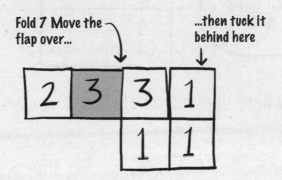

Fold **7** Move the flap over...

...then tuck it behind here

7 Fold the left hand 3 over onto the right hand 3, then tuck the end of the flap behind the 1 on the top right.

If you end up with a square showing all four 1s then give yourself a cheer! It's time to celebrate by sticking a small bit of tape on the top right 1 and folding it over the top so it sticks to the 2 on the back.

Bit of tape folded over the top

YAHOO! Well done me!

Here's where the fun starts!

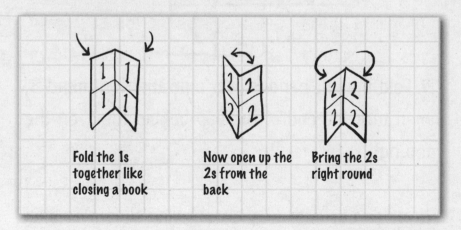

Fold the 1s together like closing a book

Now open up the 2s from the back

Bring the 2s right round

Fold the 1s together as if you're closing a book. The 2s should be on the outside. Now open the flexagon up from the back keeping the 2s in front of you.

Bring the sides right round and fold the 2s together as if you're closing a book again, then open it up from the back. (The first few times you do this, be careful not to tear it!) The 3s should appear, and if you look on the back you'll see the 4s!

But how do you find the secret faces?

Fold the flexagon back the other way until you've got the 1s at the front. Now fold the top half down onto the bottom half. You'll see two upside-down 2s. Fold them downwards, and the 'x's will appear!

Oooh!

Finally, fold the bottom two 'x's right round to the back, then lift up the top two 'x's.

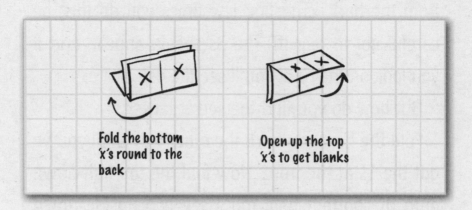

Fold the bottom 'x's round to the back

Open up the top 'x's to get blanks

You've found the blank squares, so now you can draw your alien!

When you do the trick on Nancy, show her the alien, then quickly fold the flexagon back so the 1s are showing, and then show her how to get to see the 2s, 3s and 4s. Once she's used to opening the flexagon like a book, it will take her a long time to realize that sometimes it can open the other way!

PING!

While we're busy cutting and folding paper, try this lovely little trick with a strip of paper and two paperclips. It works really well with a £10 note if you've got one!

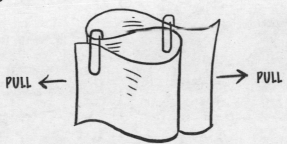

PULL ←   → PULL

Fold the paper, and fix the clips on, then pull the ends apart and see what happens!

COIN TRICKS

The Cup of Flames

This is a nice little trick you can play with coins, but Urgum the Axeman and Grizelda the Grisly like to make things a bit more dangerous…

"Not again!" moaned Urgum the Axeman.

He was sitting at a stone table looking at metal cup full of bubbling fire juice. He had been playing a game with Grizelda the Grisly all afternoon and lost every time.

"Go on Urgum, drink up!" laughed Grizelda.

Urgum snatched up the cup and drank the juice down as fast as he could. He took a deep breath and waited. Slowly he started to smile.

"It doesn't work on me any more!" he said. "I can't feel a thi—"

KAZOOSH!

Two jets of smoke shot out of his ears, and flames blasted out of his mouth.

"What was that you were saying?" asked Grizelda.

"Nothing," mumbled Urgum as a little wisp of steam floated up from his nose.

"Do you want to play again?" asked Grizelda.

"I'll play," growled Urgum. "You'll HAVE to lose sometime!"

But Grizelda never did lose, because she was using a clever little numbers trick!

The game had thirteen cups. Twelve cups were full of water, and the last one had the fire juice.

Urgum and Grizelda took it in turns to drink from the cups. They were each allowed to drink one, two or three cups of water. Whoever was left with the last cup had to drink the fire juice!

Grizelda's trick is that she always let Urgum have the first turn.

If Urgum drank ONE cup, she drank THREE.

If Urgum drank TWO cups, she drank TWO.

If Urgum drank THREE cups, she drank ONE.

That way, Urgum always ended up with the last cup!

The reason this works is that every time Urgum and Grizelda take a turn, between them they drink four cups.

When Urgum starts there are 13 full cups on the table.

When Urgum has his next turn there are 13-4 = 9 full cups.

One his next turn there are 9-4 = 5 full cups.

And finally, when Urgum has his last turn, there are 5-4 cups which just leaves 1 cup … and it's the fire juice!

If you want to try this trick, put a line of 13 coins or counters on the table. You and a friend take turns to pick up one, two or three coins. The loser is the person who picks up the last coin! If you do what Grizelda did, you will always win!

You don't have to start with 13 coins. You can pick

any number from the four times table then add 1. You could try 17, 21, 25, 29...

Although this game is easy to win, it's also quite easy for the other person to see how you're doing it. The next game we're going to look at also involves picking up coins, but whoever you're playing against is going to find it much harder!

The Last Coin

Set out six coins in three rows like this.

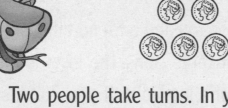

Two people take turns. In your turn, you choose one row, then take as many coins as you like from it. *The winner is the person who picks up the last coin.*

We're going to play against Daz. The trick is that if we let Daz go first, we should always win! The secret is that after Daz has had his turn, we do whatever move is needed to leave either two rows of two coins or two rows with one coin each. This is how a couple of games might go:

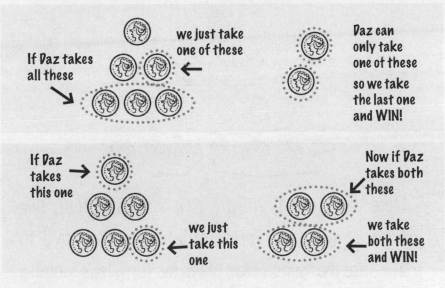

If you practise with a friend and make them go first, you'll soon see how to win every game.

This is called a NIM game, and there are lots of different versions. If you know the maths involved, you can win almost all the time!

Let's start with four rows of 1, 3, 5 and 7 coins. The secret of winning is to divide the coins in each row into groups of 1, 2 or 4 coins.

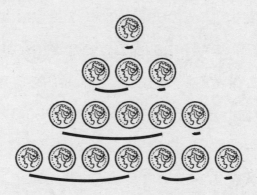

Here you'll see there are *two* groups of four, *two* groups of two and *four* single coins. We have to make sure that when Daz plays his turn, he's looking at even numbers of each group. That's what we've got at the moment, so we'll let him play.

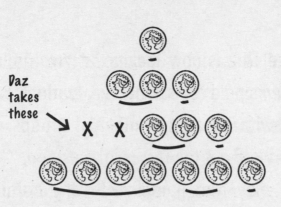

Daz takes these → X X

Daz has taken two coins from the third row. This has changed our groups! We've still got four single coins, but now we have *three* groups of two and *one* group of four. As there are an odd number of the two group and the four group, we make sure we take away one of each. The only way to do that is remove six coins from the bottom row.

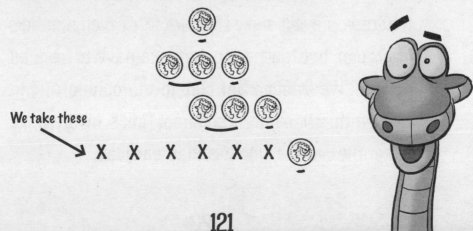

We take these → X X X X X X

You'll see Daz is now looking at *two* groups of two and *four* single coins. Whatever he does, we can leave him with an even number of groups again. Eventually we'll get the last coin!

You can play Nim games with any number of rows or coins. So long as you can make the other person face even numbers of groups, you will have control of the game!

Misere Nim

Some Nim games are called *misere,* which means that we have to make Daz pick up the last coin. In that case, we still make Daz pick from even numbers of groups, but towards the end we have to be a bit devious. We either want Daz to be looking at two rows with the same number of coins in them, or three rows with a single coin in each!

If Daz is looking at this... 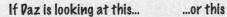 ...or this we can make him pick up the last coin!

We haven't space in this book to show you all the possible things you might have to do, but now you've seen how it works, go and find somebody and try it out!

Heads or Tails or Heads again?

You need any coin, plus a pencil and paper. You're going to toss the coin a few times and see how it lands, but before you start, show Daz this picture:

He has to choose any sequence of three results, such as TAILS HEADS HEADS, or HEADS TAILS HEADS. You then choose a different sequence for yourself.

Start tossing the coin and keep track of how it lands each time. (You might want to write it down.) The sequence that comes up first wins!

Let's say that Daz chose TAILS HEADS TAILS and you chose TAILS TAILS HEADS. This is what might happen:

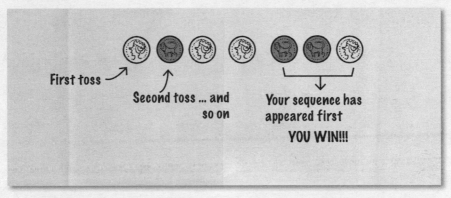

First toss

Second toss ... and so on

Your sequence has appeared first
YOU WIN!!!

Here's the good bit. If you pick the right sequence, then you will win far more than Daz will!

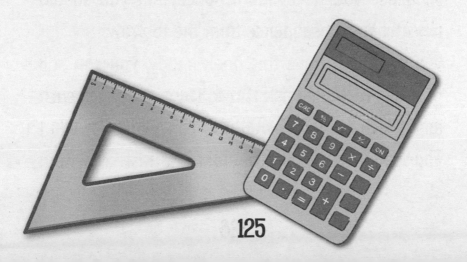

Here is the same picture of the eight sequences. Whichever one Daz picks, follow the arrow to see which sequence YOU should choose!

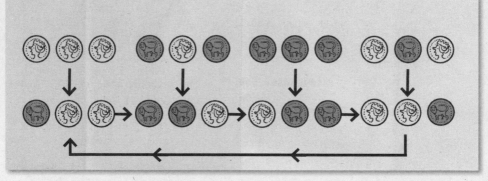

Remember this pattern of arrows, so that you don't have to turn the page and check which sequence you need. You'll notice that you should never choose a sequence from the top row!

If you don't have this book handy, you can still play this trick. Just ask Daz to say a sequence such as HEADS-HEADS-TAILS. You can work out what your sequence should be. Take the last coin from

Daz's sequence, so here you would be left with HEADS HEADS. Then you add a coin on the front that's different to the last coin, so you'd end up with TAILS HEADS HEADS.

It's hard to believe how well this trick works until you try it! If you want to test it out, pretend you're Daz and choose one of the eight sequences, then see which sequence you would choose. Start tossing a coin and see if you would have won. You'll be amazed!

It's the Same Old Tails...

It's been a long night at the Last Chance Saloon, and Brett Shuffler has been checking how much money he's got left.

THE LAST CHANCE SALOON

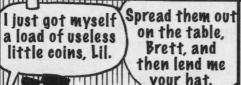

I just got myself a load of useless little coins, Lil.

Spread them out on the table, Brett, and then lend me your hat.

Can you see anything, Lil?

Not a thing! Now shuffle the coins around.

Now I'll just take a few then you count up how many tails are left.

You still can't see?

Nope. Now I put my coins back on the table and I bet that I got the same number of tails that you have.

Hey I got four tails and so have you! Mercy me!

And that was all done without looking, Brett!

So how did Lil manage to get the same number of tails without looking?

It's simple! When Brett first puts his coins on the table, she counts up how many tails she can see. After that, she doesn't need to see anything else!

Brett shuffles the coins around, but he mustn't turn any over. Then however many tails Lil saw, she carefully slides that same number of coins off the table into her hand *again being careful not to turn any over!* (So if she saw five tails, she takes five coins, but it doesn't matter which five she takes.)

While she's holding the coins under the table she turns them ALL over, then when she puts them back, she will have the same number of tails as Brett!

How does this work?

Suppose Lil can see three tails, then she removes three coins. Now suppose they just happen to be the three tails. There will be no tails left on the table. Then when Lil turns her coins over and puts them back, she won't have any tails either!

But now suppose Lil sees three tails, and removes two heads and one tail. That will leave two tails on the table. When she turns over her coins, her two heads and one tail will turn into one head and two tails. Once again, she has the same number of tails.

This works with any number of tails on the table, and it doesn't matter how many of them she picks!

The Coin Collection

Get a mixture of coins and lay them out in a line. They can be in any order but the coins at each end should both be low value (e.g. 1p).

You and Nancy take turns to pick a coin off the end of the line. You can pick your coin from either end. Keep going until all the coins have been taken. Of course, the idea is that your coins are worth more than Nancy's!

The Secret: If there is an *even* number of coins, then you should go first. Imagine the coins are coloured black and white alternately along the row. (If you want to practise this, you could lay the coins out heads-tails-heads-tails etc.) Add up the value of all the black coins, and then add up the value of all the white coins. Whichever value is higher, then make sure those are the coins you pick up!

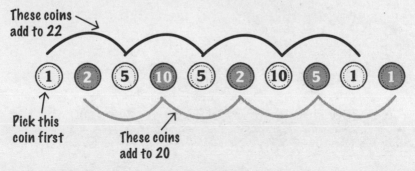

These coins add to 22

Pick this coin first

These coins add to 20

Here you'll see the white coins add to 22, and the black coins add to 20. For your first turn you need to pick up the white coin at the end. This leaves a black coin at both ends, so Nancy has to pick a black coin up. After Nancy has had her turn, always pick your coin from the same end as she did. You'll end up with all the white coins and win!

If there is an *odd* number of coins, then let Nancy go first and pick up a small coin at the end. This will leave you facing an even number of coins, so divide them into black and white, then play as before.

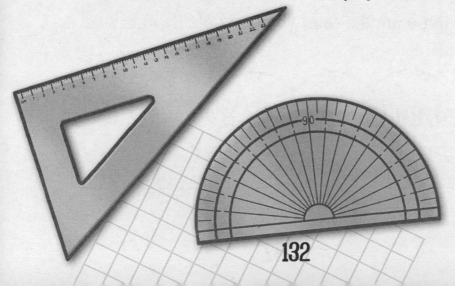

NUMBER TRICKS

It's always handy to know a few number tricks because numbers are the most powerful thing in the universe. It's true. Do aliens need to wear socks? Do they drink lemonade? Do they understand the offside rule in football? No! In fact they probably don't even know what we're talking about, but there's one thing they will know for certain. $1+1=2$

If you don't believe how powerful numbers are, then get ready to see how we can use them to stop an alien invasion!

The Mind Reader

This is a really freaky trick. You can try it on somebody sitting across the room, but we've just spotted the

Evil Gollarks from the planet Zog approaching in their battle cruiser. They want revenge because we interrupted their picnic back on page 85! Don't worry, we can use this trick to scare them off!

We're going to send the Gollarks some instructions. Here's what they have to do.

• Write down a three digit number. *The digits should all be different, the biggest should be at the front and the smallest at the back.*

• Write the number underneath, but reverse the digits so the smallest digit is at the front and the biggest is at the back.

• Take the bottom number away from the top number, and write the answer underneath.

We can now give them a nasty surprise!

No, it wasn't a lucky guess!

The Secret: It doesn't matter what three digit number the Gollarks start with, two strange things always happen.

The answer will ALWAYS have a 9 in the middle.

The first digit and the last digit will ALWAYS add up to 9.

So if the Gollarks say the first digit is 2, then the last digit has to be 7 because $2+7 = 9$.

Try this yourself! Pick any three digit number (different digits, biggest at the front) , turn it round and take away. You'll get 9 in the middle, and the first and last digits add to make 9.

Good isn't it?

But the Gollarks haven't given up yet. We're going to have to scare them even more!

This is what we tell them to do...

- Turn the answer round and write it underneath.

- Finally add up the last two answers.

We can tell them the final total even though we haven't seen ANYTHING!

This is what the Gollarks' sum looked like when it was finished:

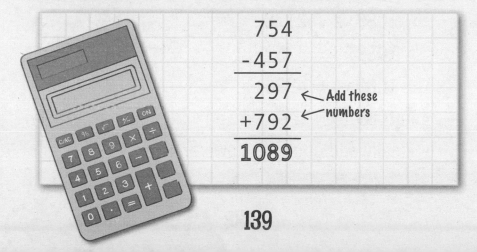

$$754$$
$$-457$$
$$297 \leftarrow \text{Add these}$$
$$+792 \leftarrow \text{numbers}$$
$$1089$$

It wouldn't have mattered what number the Gollarks started with, and we didn't even need to ask what the first digit of the first answer was! The answer was always going to be 1089, but why? We could give you all sorts of clever explanations, but the nicest reason is because 1089 is WEIRD.

Why is 1089 weird?

To start with, you can learn the 1089 times table in about 20 seconds. Here's the first bit...

$$1089 \times 1 = 1089$$
$$1089 \times 2 = 2178$$
$$1089 \times 3 = 3267$$
$$1089 \times 4 = 4356$$
$$1089 \times 5 = \ldots$$

Can you see the pattern? Just look down the column of answers. The first digits go 1, 2, 3, 4 … and the last digits go 9, 8, 7, 6…

Here's the fun bit. When you get to 1089×9 you get 9801. It's turned backwards! In fact look at this lot:

$$1089 \times 9 = 9801$$
$$10989 \times 9 = 98901$$
$$109989 \times 9 = 989901$$
$$1099989 \times 9 = 9899901$$

Here's another odd thing. If you get a calculator and work out 33×33 you get 1089. If you work out 333×333 you get 110889. What do you think you'll get for 3333×3333?

If you have a calculator with a long screen, put in 1/1089. You get 0·00091827364554637281 … can you see all the numbers in the 9 times table?

And finally, if you put in 1/9801, here's what you get:

0·000102030405060708091011121314 15…

The Fibonacci trick

Draw out six boxes in a column, then a slightly bigger box at the bottom. (We've labelled the boxes A–G so we can explain what's happening, but you don't have to do that.)

Daz puts his numbers here

Ask Daz to pick two numbers. They can be any numbers he likes, but it's easier if they are both under 10. One nice way to do this is to get your NINE PACK of cards, shuffle them up and let Daz pick two of them. (Ace counts as 1.)

This is what Daz has to do:

Write his numbers in the top two boxes, one in each. They can be either way round.

Add the top two boxes up and write the answer in box C.

Add B+C and put the answer in D.

Add C+D and put the answer in E.

At this point you write a secret prediction on a big piece of paper, then fold it into a hat and make Daz wear it.

Add D+E and put the answer in F.

Finally, Daz adds up all six numbers and puts the answer in the big box G.

You just multiply this number x4 to get answer.

Tell Daz to take the hat off and look at the number you wrote on it!

The Secret: Just see what number Daz writes in the fifth box down (that's box E) and multiply it by 4!

It doesn't matter what two numbers Daz starts with, so long as he gets his sums right, you'll have written the right answer.

This Trick has a BIG Version!

Draw out a column of 10 boxes, then put one more big box at the bottom. Ask Daz to put two numbers in the top two boxes, then fill in the other boxes as before, adding together the last two boxes each time. Finally he puts the total of the top 10 boxes into the bottom box ... but you wrote your prediction after he filled in the seventh box!

The Secret: The total should be whatever number is in the seventh box ×11.

How to Multiply a Two-Digit Number by 11 Quickly!

This is handy if you're doing the big version of the Fibonacci trick. Suppose you need to know 53×11, you just add the two digits and put the answer in the middle! So 5+3 = 8, and that means the answer is 583.

Just be careful if the digits add up to more than 9.

Suppose you have 76×11, you get 7+6 = 13. You put the 3 in the middle, then add the 1 on to the 7 so you get 836.

The Diabolical Mirror Number

So there you are one morning having a nice wash and looking in the mirror when … arghhh! What has happened to your face? Your lovely features have got all wrinkly, your hair looks like old newspaper and your nose is sticking out like an ice-cream cone.

"Har har!" says the mirror.

Only it isn't the mirror. It's your arch enemy Professor Fiendish, who has taken the mirror away and is looking at you through a hole in the wall.

"Give me back my mirror," you say crossly.

"Not until you have solved my diabolical MIRROR NUMBER challenge!" he says with an evil chuckle.

You have no choice. If you want to see your gorgeous face again, you'll have to do what he wants.

"I will give you a set of numbers, and you have to turn them into mirror numbers," he says. "If you fail then I'll cover your mirror in blobs of stripy toothpaste so it looks like horrible spots and you will never dare to look at yourself again!"

How very ghastly.

The professor writes some numbers on the wall: 37 48 78 52.

"Hurry up!" he says. "Or the mirror gets it."

Mirror numbers are the same forwards as they are backwards, and they can also be called *palindromes*. 55, 141, 2882 and 1670761 are all mirror numbers.

There's a nice little trick that turns any two digit number into a mirror number. All you do is turn the number round and add, then if necessary turn the answer round and add again. Keep going until you get a mirror number!

"Well?" says the professor. "I'm waiting!"

You get a pencil and attack the professor's numbers. Luckily you happen to be very clever, and you're finished in a flash.

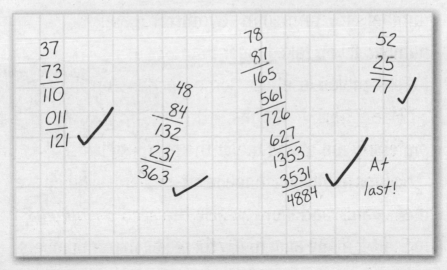

37
73
___
110
011
___
121 ✓

48
84
___
132
231
___
363 ✓

78
87
___
165
561
___
726
627
____
1353
3531
____
4884 ✓ At last!

52
25
___
77 ✓

"There!" you say. "All done. Now give me back my mirror."

"Never," says the professor. "You took far too long!"

"Oh yeah?" you say casually. "I'm a lot faster than you!"

"Never!" cries the professor. "Give me some numbers and watch me. I'm a genius."

"Very well," you say. "I'll just give you ONE number to turn into a mirror number. If you take longer than I did then you lose!"

"Har har!" laughs the professor. "Go ahead then."

So you give him one number, then stand back and watch the fun. After many long hours there is a horrible burning cheese smell as the professor's brain starts to melt.

"Mercy!" cries the professor. He hands back your mirror then runs away with green smoke pouring out of his ears.

The Secret: every two digit number will make a mirror number. Most of them come out quite quickly, but for some of them you might need up to six sums before a mirror number appears. However there are two diabolical numbers that take a VERY long time! So when the professor asks you for a number, here's what you say: 89. (Or you can say 98.)

89 will make a mirror number, but not before the professor is begging for mercy. It takes 24 sums which get longer and longer and harder and harder until finally you get this: 8813200023188!

But of course, if the professor makes one tiny mistake then he'll miss it and he could go on for EVER!

495 and 6174

Here are two numbers that appear by magic!

495 and 6174 are called Kaprekar numbers after the man who invented this trick.

Get your NINE PACK of cards and ask Daz to pick three of them. You're going to use the three digits he picked.

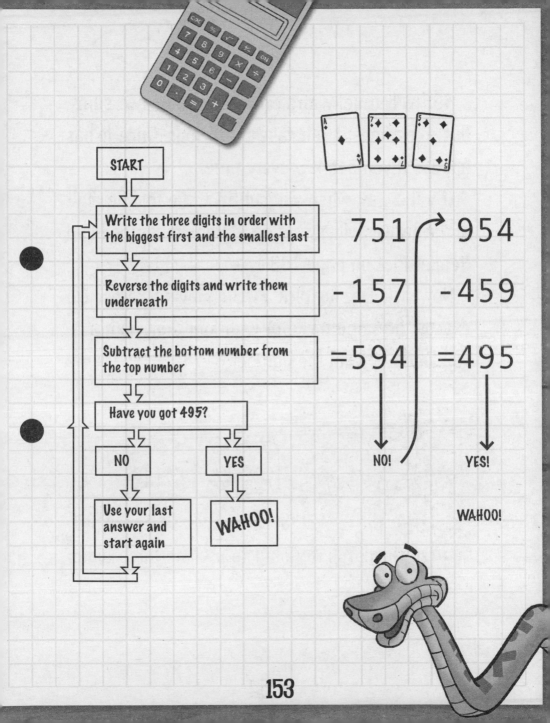

START

Write the three digits in order with the biggest first and the smallest last

Reverse the digits and write them underneath

Subtract the bottom number from the top number

Have you got 495?

NO

YES

Use your last answer and start again

WAHOO!

$$751$$
$$-157$$
$$=594$$

NO!

$$954$$
$$-459$$
$$=495$$

YES!

WAHOO!

153

495 will usually turn up after one or two sums, but sometimes it can take up to four. Once it has appeared you get 495 every time!

(By the way, when you subtract, the middle digit of the answer will always be 9! Remember the Mind Reader trick on page 133.)

Now ask Daz to pick FOUR playing cards. Do exactly the same trick but with four digit numbers. You'll end up with the number 6174!

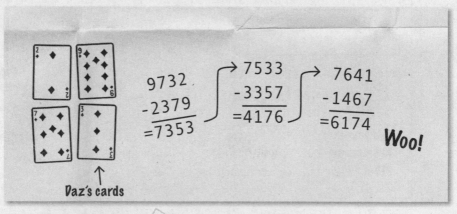

$$9732$$
$$-2379$$
$$=7353$$

$$\rightarrow 7533$$
$$-3357$$
$$=4176$$

$$\rightarrow 7641$$
$$-1467$$
$$=6174$$

Woo!

↑
Daz's cards

This should never take more than seven sums, and you can check each sum as you go along with another little trick!

If you add up the digits in each answer, you should get either 18 or 27. The answer in the first sum is 7353. Let's check it: 7+3+5+3 =18 so it's right!

The Mystery Animal

Here's a very quick trick to try on yourself or a friend.

Think of a number between 1-9.
Add 1
Multiply it by 9.
Add 1
Add together the two digits of your answer

You now should have an even number! If not then go back and check your sums.

Divide your answer by 2.
Convert your answer into a letter:

1=A
2=B
3=C
4=D
5=E
6=F
7=G
8=H
I=9

Think of an animal that begins with your answer!
Turn to page 187. (If you're doing this trick to a friend, wave the page at them!)

Here's a chapter to get Urgum the Axeman all excited!

Where's this dragon then? I'm ready!

If you get a little strip of paper and fold it in half, then open it out into a right angle, you get this:

It might not look very exciting, but it's got a good name. It's a *first order dragon curve!*

Now suppose your strip is a bit longer and you fold it, then fold it over again. When you open it out, you get a *second order dragon curve.* The little arrow shows where it opens up to make the new curve.

That's not a dragon!

If you try it with longer and longer strips, the shapes get more and more complicated. Here come the third and fourth dragon curves...

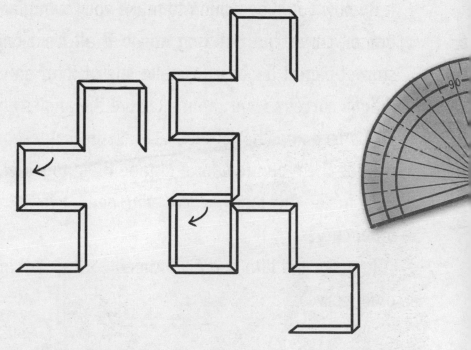

You'll notice that when we get to the fourth curve, a little square shape has appeared. This is quite important. The odd thing about the dragon curve is that it doesn't matter how many times we fold and unfold the paper, it never tries to cross over itself, it just makes neat little squares.

By now you'll be itching to make your own giant dragon curve, but don't try to do it all from one strip of paper! It's best to make lots of third order dragon curves so you can make sure the angles are all perfect and the lengths are all the same. You then lie them on the floor and tape them together.

To make the fourth curve you need two third order curves.

To make the fifth curve you need 2×2 = 4 third order curves.

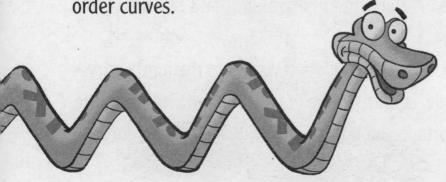

Here comes the sixth dragon curve...

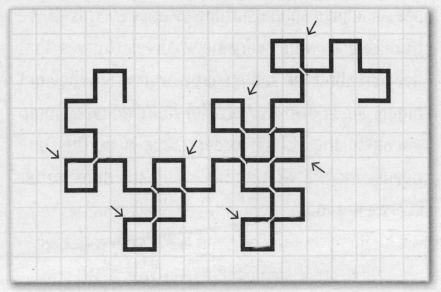

It takes 2×2×2 = 8 of the third order curves to make the sixth dragon curve! The little arrows show where the third order curves start and finish.

Oooh!

You have to use your imagination, but can you see an animal shape starting to appear? This shape gets clearer with every new curve! (Curves that keep creating the same shape even when they get bigger are known as *fractals*.) We're going to jump ahead to the TENTH order curve now. This one needs $2 \times 2 \times 2 \times 2 \times 2 \times 2 \times 2 = 128$ third order curves, but look...

That's more like it!

WITH A LITTLE BIT OF LUCK!

There are all sorts of games where you pick cards or roll dice or toss coins, and if you're lucky then you win. But if you know a bit of maths magic, you'll be even luckier!

For these tricks we need something to use as prizes, so we'll ask Binkie Smallbrains to go to the bank and get £1,000,000 out in pennies and pile them up on a table for us.

What fun!

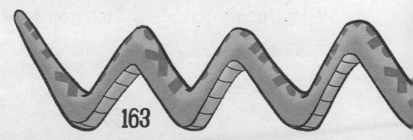

When we do the tricks, we'll play for pennies off the pile and see who wins the most!

(If you haven't got a rich friend then you can use Monopoly money, or you can play for counters, or you can just keep a score of your winnings on a piece of paper. You could even go round all your drawers and get everybody's socks out and put them in a pile to use for prizes. How lovely.)

Unfair on Who?

Tell Binkie that you're going to toss a coin and you have up to THREE chances to make it land on heads.

1 If you get heads on your first go, you win 1p. If you don't get heads then you try again.

2 If you get heads on your second go, you win 1p. If you don't get heads then you have one last chance!

3 If you get heads on your third go, you win 1p…
BUT if you don't get heads after three goes then
Binkie wins 5p!

That sounds unfair, doesn't it?

You get three goes to win 1p or else I win 5p? Then I'll win more!

No he won't. The game is unfair … but it's unfair
to Binkie! This game does rely on a bit of luck, but
if you play eight times, Binkie should only win once,
and you should win seven times. That's because
your chance of tossing three times and NOT getting
heads is $\frac{1}{2} \times \frac{1}{2} \times \frac{1}{2} = \frac{1}{8}$. This means that for every time
Binkie wins 5p, you will win seven lots of 1p, so you
get 7p.

Remember that all these games rely on *probability*. In other words you can't be certain how many times you'll win or lose, the maths just gives you a rough idea. For this game, if you play eight times you might be unlucky and find Binkie wins two or more lots of 5p. But if you play maybe 100 times, you should end up winning more than he will!

The Confused Coins

This trick is so simple, and yet so strange! You'll need somebody that Binkie can trust to help you, so we'll invite the Duchess in.

The Secret: if you always say tails, you should win this bet two times out of three! The confusing bit is that if the Duchess throws two tails you ask her to throw again. It looks like you're getting rid of some of the chances of getting tails! What really happens is this:

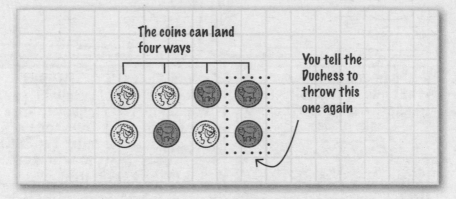

The coins can land four ways

You tell the Duchess to throw this one again

The two coins can land in four different ways, but if you don't let the Duchess keep the two tails, there are only three ways left. When the Duchess shows that one of the coins is heads, two of these ways have the other coin as tails, so tails is the best thing to say!

The Dodgy Dice!

This trick needs four special dice. You can either cut these shapes out of card and fold them, or get four normal dice and cover them in stickers with the right numbers on.

```
      3
  4   5   4
      3
      5
```

```
      6
      0
  6   6   0
      6
```

```
      7
  7   7   1
      1
      1
```

```
          2
          2
      2   2   8
          8
```

Let Binkie look at these dice. He'll find that the numbers on each one add up to 24.

Binkie can choose any die he likes, then you choose a die. You both throw them. Whoever gets the higher number wins 1p.

> That seems fair enough!

169

Amazingly, you should be able to win twice as often as Binkie does!

The Secret: Here are the dice. Whichever one Binkie chooses to throw, you use the next one along. (Follow the arrows!)

The easiest way to remember this is to look at the highest number on the dice. Whatever Binkie's highest number is, you use the next one up unless he uses the "8" die in which case you use the "5" die.

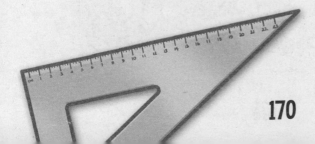

THE MISSING CENT

Sometimes it's hard to tell if somebody has done a magic trick or not, and this can lead to big trouble!

City:	Chicago Illinois USA
Place:	Luigi's Diner, Upper Main Street
Date:	31 January 1929
Time:	10:41 p.m.

The seven shady men in hats were sitting around the table in Luigi's diner. They all finished off their drinks, then pushed their dirty plates away and patted their stomachs.

"Oof!" they all said together. They were sounding very full.

A worried-looking head popped up from behind the counter. It was Luigi, who always hid himself away while the seven men were eating.

"Hey Luigi, bring the bill," said Blade, who had the blackest hat. "That was one great dinner."

"Glad you liked it boys!" said Luigi.

In fact Luigi was VERY glad, because if the men didn't like it, then things could have got nasty. He hurried over with the bill.

"The pasta pie and the bottle of wine comes to 70 cents," said Luigi.

"That's good," said Weasel, the littlest of the men. "Seventy cents between seven of us means each man has to pay … er…"

"Ten cents each," said Numbers. He was the quiet guy who could do the sums.

"That's good," said Luigi. "Because I sure hate it when you guys all start arguing."

"Hey, I never start arguing!" said One-Finger Jimmy. He pointed his one finger across the table. "It's usually him."

"Me?" snapped Half-Smile. "I don't start arguments, but I sure can finish them."

"That's better than Porky over there!" laughed Weasel rudely.

He pointed at Blade's brother who was the biggest

man. "The only thing he ever finishes is other people's lunch!"

"Me?" said Porky. He was picking up the plates one by one and giving them a final lick. "I'm just being tidy."

"Yeah, he's being tidy," Blade warned them. "So you say sorry, or you'll regret it."

"You'll be the one that's sorry," snarled Chainsaw Charlie, then he opened his chainsaw-shaped suitcase and pulled out a chainsaw-shaped chainsaw.

The men all jumped to their feet. Weasel pulled his secret shoe-gun from his shoe. Half-Smile pulled his bull whip from under his hat. Numbers pulled his finger from his nose.

Luigi ducked down behind the counter again. He was expecting a big fight, but suddenly a miracle happened. The door opened and in came a woman wrapped in a cloud of perfume. She was wearing tall heels and a spotty jacket.

"It's Dolly Snowlips!" gasped the men.

"Hi boys," said Dolly. "I sure hope you're not going to fight in front of a lady?"

"Er … no!" said the men.

"Pardon us ma'am," said Weasel blushing nervously. "We were just finishing our dinner."

"You eat with a gun in your hand?" said Dolly. "Well mercy me. I thought that grown-ups used a fork."

The men put their weapons away then Luigi hurried over to collect their money. Each man passed him ten cents.

Dolly looked at the bill.

"I see the wine was thirteen cents", said Dolly. "I just had a bit of luck with some dodgy dice, so I'll treat you to that!"

So Dolly gave Luigi an extra thirteen cents.

"Thank you kindly ma'am," said the men.

Luigi went and put seventy cents in the till, but he was still holding the money that Dolly gave him.

"I better give this thirteen cents back to you guys," he said.

Each man held out his hand and Luigi put a one cent coin into it.

"I got six cents left," said Luigi. "How do I split it between the seven of you?"

"Why don't you all give Luigi a tip?" asked Dolly.

The men agreed.

"Wow, six cents," muttered Luigi. "Now I can take my mom on that trip to Europe I always promised her."

"So everyone's happy!" chuckled Dolly as she walked over and opened the door. "That's good, but the funny thing is that you guys paid 70 cents to start with. But then all seven of you each got a cent back so you ended up paying 63 cents. Luigi has got 6 cents so that makes a total of 69 cents. It's just a thought but ... *who's got the missing cent?*"

As soon as Dolly left, the seven men turned on each other.

"Hey Blade!" shouted Weasel. "Have you guys pulled a trick?"

"No way, it's just the sort of sneaky think you'd do," snapped Blade.

"I don't trust any of you!" roared Chainsaw. "In fact I don't even trust ME…"

Once again the men pulled out their weapons and Luigi dived behind the counter.

So where do YOU think the extra cent disappeared to?

ANSWER

This is an old trick which has fooled people for years. You need to work out what the gangsters' final bill came to. To start with the bill was 70 cents, but Dolly paid 13 cents so the final bill was 70-13 = 57 cents. As they paid 70 cents and then got 7 cents back, in total they paid 63 cents. This includes 57 cents for the bill plus 6 cents for Luigi. 63 cents = 57 cents+6 cents.

WHAT SORT OF PERSON ARE YOU?

Y ou can try this on your friends!

You need to write out your birthday then turn it into one of these magic numbers:

1 2 3 4 5 6 7 8 9 11 22

Suppose you were born on May 15th 2003. Write it out like this: 15/5/03. You add up all the digits 1+5+5+0+3 − 14. Unfortunately 14 isn't on the list, so you keep going. You add up 1+4 = 5. That's your magic number!

If your number comes out as 10, then that's not a magic number. You have to do 1+0 = 1 and that's your magic number! If your number is 11 or 22, you don't add 1+1 or 2+2 because these are

"master numbers" which make you *very special.*
Oooh!

Now have a look and see what you're like!

Magic Number

1 Bossy, impulsive and full of yourself

2 Affectionate, shy, deep thinker

3 Party animal, enthusiastic and probably rather irritating

4 Reliable worker and good organizer

5 Adventurous and restless, you'll try anything once

6 Very clean, very tidy and slightly scary!

7 A loner whose mind is away with the fairies

8 Money driven and ruthless

9 Amazing imagination, rarely looks smart (So you're a hippy ... *yeah groovy man!*)

11 Artistic, inspiring but impractical ... in other words you're a bit weird

22 Determined, practical and you're on a mission to improve the world. YAY!

Y ou hold two flat bits of card out in front of you and then suddenly they turn into a magic ball!

This is one of the nicest toys in maths. The ball is actually a *dodecahedron* and it has 12 faces, 20 corners and 30 edges. Each face is a perfect five-sided *pentagon*. All you need to make it are two special shapes cut out of card and a big elastic band.

Start by drawing a pentagon on a piece of card. It should be about 12 cm across, although if you're brave you can try to make a bigger one! Some computer art programmes will draw a perfect pentagon for you, so print one out and then trace it onto your card. Otherwise if you've got a set of compasses and ruler you can draw a pentagon yourself.

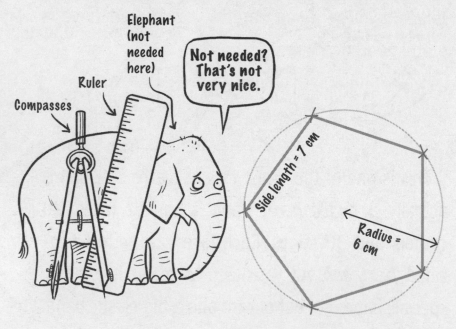

Elephant (not needed here)

Not needed? That's not very nice.

Ruler

Compasses

Side length = 7 cm

Radius = 6 cm

Open the compasses up to 6 cm and draw a circle. Then open your compasses a bit wider to 7 cm. Stick the point on the circle then swizzle it round to make two marks on the circle. Stick the point on one of the marks and swizzle it again, and then do it again until you have five marks round the edge of the circle. Join them up with the pencil and ruler. If you've been careful you should have a pretty good pentagon!

Draw in all the diagonals to make a star.

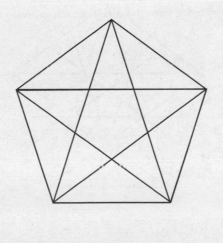

You'll see there's another pentagon in the middle, so draw in its diagonals to make a little star.

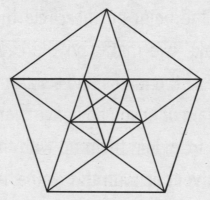

Now you have to make the lines of the little star longer, so they touch the sides of the big pentagon.

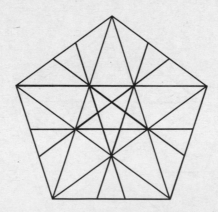

Next you need to chop out these triangles:

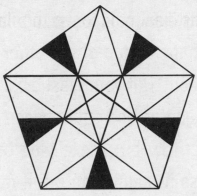

Finally you end up with this shape, and you need to make two of them:

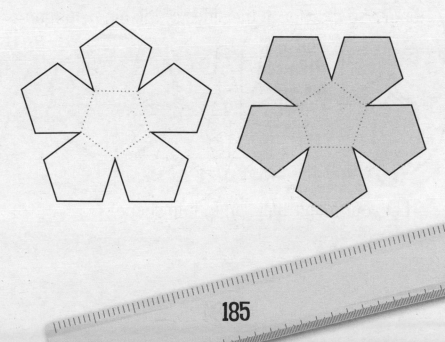

Fold along the dotted lines one at a time then open them up again to loosen the flaps up.

Put one shape on top of the other so that all ten corners stick out. Put your elastic band around both shapes so it goes in and out between all the corners. (This is the tricky bit! The elastic band has to be quite tight, so it might ping off. If it does then you can ask your elephant to go and get it.)

So you DID need me after all!

Elastic band goes all the way round

Let your magic ball spring into shape!

HOW TO CHECK A TILL RECEIPT QUICKLY

Although it's really nice having an elephant to help you with your tricks, you do need to feed it and keep it happy. Unfortunately there's only one shop we know that sells elephant stuff.

FIENDISH ELEPHANT STORES

Oh no! The shop smells of mouldy sprouts, and that can only mean one thing. Professor Fiendish is behind the counter! Watch out, because he's sure to play a mean try on you.

"Welcome!" he says with an evil grin. "Pick what you want off the shelves then I'll add it up."

So you get everything you need, and walk over to the till.

"Make sure you put the right prices in!" you warn him. "I'm watching!"

"Of course!" he says.

Beep Beep Beep Beep! goes the till.

Everything looks correct so far.

"Let's see how much you owe me," says the professor.

But just as he pushes the TOTAL button on the till, you notice him click on a secret swindle switch.

BING! goes the till.

"That will be £246.27," he says.

"What?" you gasp. "That's a lot just for some food and washing things."

"See for yourself," says the professor.

He passes over the paper till receipt with everything on it.

Fiendish Elephant Stores

Straw pies	£4.30
Bamboo sticks	£3.25
Big mushrooms	£1.90
Grass stew	£2.70
Coconut milk	£2.09
Mud soup	£0.75
Banana crisps	£0.40
Huge shower cap	£5.49
Giant rubber duck	£7.00
Bucket	£4.99
Soap	£0.60
Trunk polish	£3.50
Eyebrow pencil	£0.90
Toe nail varnish	£5.45
TOTAL	£246.27

"Hmm," you say. "That doesn't look right. I'm going to check it!"

"You haven't time," says the professor. "I'm closing in ten seconds!"

"That's all the time I need," you say, being very cool.

"What?" gasps the professor. "But you haven't even got a calculator!"

"I don't need one," you say.

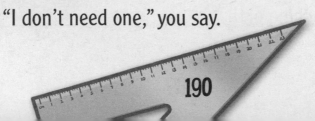

190

The professor watches amazed as you quickly look down the list of numbers, and then fold the paper in half. You do a quick bit of counting and then...

"It should come to about £43," you tell him.

"Eh? What? No it shouldn't!" says the professor.

"Yes it should, and I can prove it to you."

You reach over to the till, and click the secret swindle switch off, then you push the TOTAL button.

BING! The till now says £43.32.

"Sorry, but I've got to go," you say putting the money on the counter. "I've got a hungry elephant waiting!"

So how did you beat the professor and his cheating till?

If you want to check a receipt quickly, there are two things to do.

Add up the pounds, and ignore the pennies. Usually with shop receipts, the pounds are all small numbers less than 10, so it's not too hard. On this receipt we get £36.

Fold the list of items in half, then count up how many items are on one side. Here we get 7 items.

Huge shower cap	£5.49
Giant rubber duck	£7.00
Bucket	£4.99
Soap	£0.60
Trunk polish	£3.50
Eyebrow pencil	£0.90
Toe nail varnish	£5.45
TOTAL	£246.27

Add the two numbers together! £36+£7 = £43.

This works on most shop receipts, and your answer will never be very far out. The only thing you have to watch out for is when the receipt has discounts or negative numbers, but with a bit of practise this won't be a problem. And if you find a mistake, this trick might even save you some money!

THE DUCHESS'S MISSING HEAD!

Oh dear, there's a bit of a problem at Fogsworth Manor.

The Duchess had organized an artist to come and paint the whole family in the garden. She had spent days getting ready and looking her best, and then she had sat for hours pulling her poshest face so that in hundreds of years her great-great-great-grandchildren could admire her.

But then, just as the artist was plopping on his final blob of paint, a gust of wind blew the picture away. It landed on the grass right in front of Croak the butler, who was mowing the lawn!

RIP! SCRUNCH!

The picture was sliced into pieces, which then flew off into the pond.

"Oh no!" wailed the Duchess. "My family is drifting apart!"

"Quick Croak, collect all those bits up!" ordered the Colonel. "And Binkie, you get some tape and stick them together."

"I say, what jolly fun!" said Binkie Smallbrains. "I love jigsaw puzzles."

Soon the picture was back in one piece again.

"We've got all the bits, madam," said Croak.
"There's no gaps or anything missing."

"I can see that!" snapped the Duchess. "But Binkie
has got them all mixed up. Try again, and this time
make sure I'm in the middle!"

So Croak and Binkie had another go.

"We've done it, Mummy!" said Binkie. "We're all where we should be."

"There's just one tiny problem," muttered the Colonel. "What's happened to the Duchess's head?"

There are lots of these puzzles where pieces arrive or disappear, so let's see a few more!

The Extra Square...

A normal chessboard has 8 squares along the bottom and 8 squares up the side, so in total it has 8×8 = 64 squares.

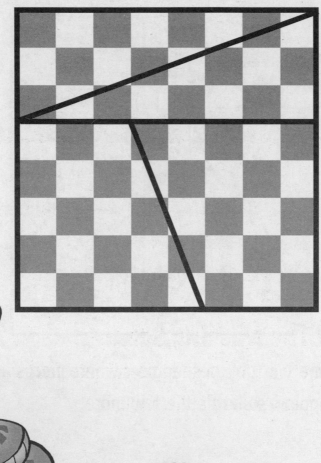

As you can see, we've chopped this one into four pieces. Now we're going to pull them apart and put them back together…

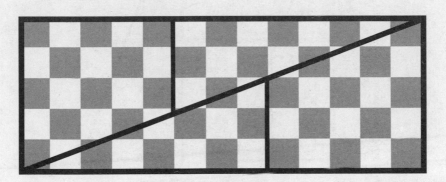

Now there are 13 squares along the bottom and 5 squares up the sides, so the total number of squares Is $13 \times 5 = 65$.

Where did the extra square come from?

…and The Missing Square…

This time we have a triangle cut into four pieces. Once again we shuffle them round…

Oh dear! You can see the same four pieces are still there, but where has the missing square gone?

...and ANOTHER Missing Square!

This time we start with a chessboard with a full 64 squares again.

We chop it *nearly* along a diagonal, then slide the top piece up. Finally we chop off the little extra triangle at the top and stick it in the space at the bottom.

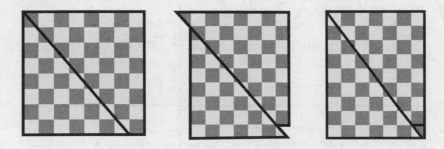

The new rectangle measures 7×9 = 63 squares. *Where has the missing square gone this time?*

If you want to know the answers, the best way is to cut out some paper and test out these shapes yourself!

You'll find that when you try make the first extra square, you can't get the four pieces to fit together exactly in the middle. With the triangles, you can't make the long edge exactly straight. With the last trick, once you've moved the top part of the shape up, all the squares along the diagonal are a tiny bit bigger than they should be.

But we're still looking for the Duchess's missing head!

Draw out a little grid of squares measuring 5×3. Put a coin on the middle square. Can you draw a path that crosses over every other square just once? The path is not allowed to go diagonally from one square to another.

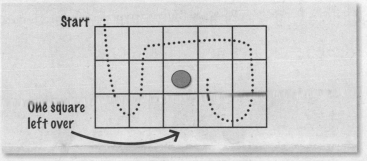

Start

One square left over

It doesn't matter where you start or how hard you try, there will always be at least one square you can't cross! But if you move the coin one place to the side...

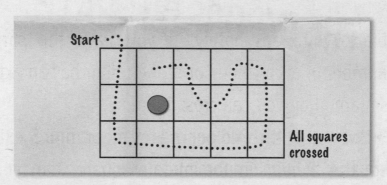

...it's easy!

You can quickly tell if you can cross all the squares or not. Imagine the squares are coloured black and white like a chess board. With our 5×3 grid, there are 8 white squares and 7 black ones.

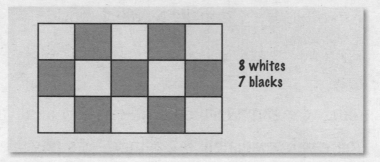

When you make a path around the board, it always has to cross over the colours black/white/

black/white alternately. If you have the same number of each colour, or if one colour has an extra square, then you can cross them all.

But … if one colour has two or more extra squares then it's impossible!

When we had the coin in the middle, if you imagine the black and white squares, we had eight whites and six blacks so it was impossible. But when we moved the coin to the side, we had seven of each colour so the puzzle was possible.

We can use this to make a baffling trick!

Draw out a big grid of 5×7 squares and show Nancy.

Nancy can put a coin on any square.

You can immediately tell Nancy if it's possible to draw a path that crosses all the other squares or not!

The Secret: Imagine the squares are all black and white as before, and the four corner squares are white. Start at any corner and see if you can get to the coin just by moving along the diagonals. If you can, then the puzzle is possible, but if not then the puzzle is impossible.

Nancy will never know how you can be so sure … unless she's read this book!

Test yourself – how many of these puzzles are impossible?

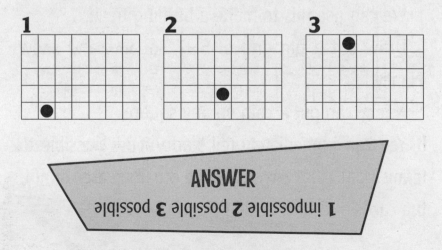

THE LAST LAUGH

Sadly we've reached the end of the book, but Thag has one final trick up his sleeve!

Lay seven cards and a joker out like this.

Here's the challenge: Can you get the joker into the middle, but still have the other cards in order round the edge?

You move the cards by sliding them one at a time into wherever the empty space is. They can't cross over each other or move diagonally, so to start with you can only move the ace, 3, 5 or 7 into the middle.

It *can* be done ... but only if you know the secret! If you want the answer, add up the numbers on the cards and turn to that page!

INDEX